823/DEF

Hertfordshire
COUNTY COUNCIL
Community Information

2 2 JUN 2006

1 7 MAY 2008

WGC

Please renew/return this item by the last date shown.

So that your telephone call is charged at local rate,
please call the numbers as set out below:

	From Area codes 01923 or 0208:	From the rest of Herts:
Renewals:	01923 471373	01438 737373
Enquiries:	01923 471333	01438 737333
Minicom:	01923 471599	01438 737599

L32

 Longman

 York Press

The Publishers would like to thank Chatto & Windus for their kind permission to reproduce extracts from *The Rise of the Novel* by Ian Watt.

Delia Dick is hereby identified as author of this work in accordance with Section 77 of the Copyright, Designs and Patents Act 1988

YORK PRESS
322 Old Brompton Road, London SW5 9JH

PEARSON EDUCATION LIMITED
Edinburgh Gate, Harlow,
Essex CM20 2JE, United Kingdom
Associated companies, branches and representatives throughout the world

First published 2000

ISBN 0–582–42478–X

Designed by Vicki Pacey
Phototypeset by Gem Graphics, Trenance, Mawgan Porth, Cornwall
Colour reproduction and film output by Spectrum Colour
Produced by Addison Wesley Longman China Limited, Hong Kong

C ONTENTS

PART ONE

INTRODUCTION

HOW TO STUDY A NOVEL

Studying a novel on your own requires self-discipline and a carefully thought-out work plan in order to be effective.

- You will need to read the novel more than once. Start by reading it quickly for pleasure, then read it slowly and thoroughly.
- On your second reading make detailed notes on the plot, characters and themes of the novel. Further readings will generate new ideas and help you to memorise the details of the story.
- Some of the characters will develop as the plot unfolds. How do your responses towards them change during the course of the novel?
- Think about how the novel is narrated. From whose point of view are events described?
- A novel may or may not present events chronologically: the time-scheme may be a key to its structure and organisation.
- What part do the settings play in the novel?
- Are words, images or incidents repeated so as to give the work a pattern? Do such patterns help you to understand the novel's themes?
- Identify what styles of language are used in the novel.
- What is the effect of the novel's ending? Is the action completed and closed, or left incomplete and open?
- Does the novel present a moral and just world?
- Cite exact sources for all quotations, whether from the text itself or from critical commentaries. Wherever possible find your own examples from the novel to back up your opinions.
- Always express your ideas in your own words.

This York Note offers an introduction to *Moll Flanders* and cannot substitute for close reading of the text and the study of secondary sources.

Moll Flanders is a novel which has always attracted controversy. There is, for instance, the question – to do with literary theory – of whether Defoe's work can actually be described as a novel; this is discussed in Parts Three, Five and Six. More immediately, there is the question of the interpretation of the character of Moll herself, a figure as memorable as any in fiction.

Defoe trumpets the shocking details of 'The Fortunes and Misfortunes Of The Famous Moll Flanders' on his title page. The reader is to learn of her many marriages – some concurrent, and one to her brother; her life as a whore and then as a thief; her transportation as a criminal to Virginia; her years of prosperity; and, finally, her penitence in old age. To be born in prison and abandoned by her deported convict mother was certainly a misfortune for the infant Moll but she has her share of good fortune too. Often married, she has several prosperous spells in her life and twelve children at various times, most surviving, but of whom we rarely hear more. Moll recognises that one of the few ways for an attractive woman to meet the need for economic survival is to exploit her charms; this she does effectively as wife, mistress and occasionally prostitute. In love as a girl with her first seducer (and with the gold he gave her) she is subsequently good-natured enough in her more extended relationships with men; however, the glamorous highwayman, her fourth husband, is the only other man who causes her to suffer the pangs of love.

Moll is a materialist; she loves money and valuable possessions well beyond the need to accumulate provision for herself in a world of harsh economics. Age and the unfortunate financial ruin and death of her last husband force Moll, she claims, into a life of crime. She is a wonderfully skilful and audacious thief – her name (or, rather, pseudonym) is known throughout the underworld by the time she is finally brought to trial for her life at the end of her eight year career of opportunist crime.

If no-one knows her real name, neither does anyone other than a very few close associates know what the notorious thief looks like. Moll's life is secretive; much as she enjoys boasting in her memoirs about her artful thefts, she is shrewd enough to maintain her privacy as best she can. She can appear sometimes a lonely figure; although she spends many years in contented domesticity, these episodes are dealt with cursorily, and it is the **picaresque** aspects of her life that Defoe dwells upon. Few other characters, therefore, are much developed, although we do meet Moll's mentors: her 'Nurse' who brings her up; her real mother; and 'Mother Midnight', Moll's 'Governess', as she calls her – a midwife, abortionist, procuress and dealer in stolen goods, who is a faithful friend to her protegée and who embraces penitence before Moll does.

The sincerity of Moll's penitence is the subject of much discussion. In his 'Preface', Defoe invites the reader to enjoy the feast of scandal he is offering, but stresses that 'the best and brightest' part of Moll's supposed narrative is that which deals with repentance. Moll herself intersperses the entertaining accounts of her adventures with a good deal of moralising, and reaffirms her true penitence in her final sentence. So the reader will want to decide whether Moll is a brazen hypocrite or sincere in her expressions of redemption. And this, for the engaged reader, may well lead to an examination of Defoe's own purpose in writing this supposed autobiography and, crucially, to an assessment of the degree of **irony** which may be detected in this fascinating work of innovative **realism**.

Part two

Summaries & Commentaries

This Note, including page references, is based on the Penguin paperback edition of *Moll Flanders*, in the Penguin Classics series, first published in 1989 and edited by David Blewett.

The title page of the first edition of *Moll Flanders* gives the date 1721, but it was actually published in January, 1722 – the first of many versions. Not such a popular success as *Robinson Crusoe*, the only one of his works of fiction to be widely known in Defoe's lifetime, *Moll Flanders* nevertheless went into a third edition before the end of the same year, and has been published many times subsequently, some eighteenth-century pirated versions appearing with additional material or reduced in length to **chapbook** format.

Most editions have been based on 'The Third Edition, Corrected'. This version, however, has recently been shown not to have been corrected by Defoe himself, but most probably suffered insensitive editing later by the publisher, with the aim of reducing his paper costs by space-saving cutting. The editor of the selected text has gone back to the first edition, as this is likely to be the closest to Defoe's original.

Synopsis

This work of fiction is presented as fact, and Defoe's 'Preface' explains that, as editor of Moll Flanders's 'Memorandums', he has moderated some of her more shocking language. The whole tale, he claims, is intended not to titillate but to serve a moral purpose by showing her ultimate repentance for her life of sin and crime.

The narrative is taken up by Moll herself, who explains that she was born in Newgate prison to a woman who was condemned to hang for the theft of some pieces of cloth. For a time she travels with a band of gypsies, but is abandoned, or runs away from them, at Colchester. Here, at the age of three, she is taken into the care of the magistrates, who have her fostered in the simple school of a sensible, pious woman who becomes fond of Moll and accepts her wish not to go into service, keeping the child with her until she dies when Moll is fourteen. The girl, who has acquired good manners and an unexpected air of refinement, has the good fortune to be taken into the prosperous family of a rich local merchant as a servant and companion to his two daughters. Always with them, she shares their education until she is seventeen or so, acquiring the necessary social accomplishments of the period. Aware of her good looks and personality, she allows herself to be drawn into an affair with the elder of the merchant's two sons. He promises her marriage and gives her money, but eventually cynically disposes of her by persuading her to marry his younger brother, who has fallen in love with her. The parents strongly disapprove of a pauper bride, but Moll's evident reluctance to marry the younger brother persuades them that she is innocent of guile in this matter. Her loss of virginity is disguised from her husband by his brother, who employs the expedient of getting the younger man so drunk that he cannot remember his wedding night.

Moll is still in love with the older brother and has little feeling for her husband, who dies after five years of marriage. Leaving her two children with their grandparents, the now wealthy widow soon finds another husband. She marries a draper, a 'gentleman-trader', and enjoys a couple of years of extravagant living with him while he squanders her money and builds up debts which force him to disappear to Paris. Moll has to escape from their creditors by moving to another part of London and changing her name to Mrs Flanders, a 'widow' as she claims.

Moll, whose second husband is, of course, still alive, puts herself on the marriage market again and soon marries a third husband, having tricked him into believing her to be very wealthy; however, although Moll has only a little money, her new husband does have quite profitable estates in America and they set up home on his plantation in Virginia, where his mother lives too. All is well, and Moll enjoys the company of her mother-in-law until, to the horror of both of them, it transpires that the old woman is Moll's own mother, reprieved from hanging many years before and transported to Virginia. Moll has unwittingly made an incestuous marriage with her own half-brother. Eventually Moll, who has been refusing to sleep with her husband, tells him what has happened. He agrees that they should part, and she returns alone to England with a valuable stock of tobacco, leaving behind her children and her husband, who is reduced to a permanent state of melancholy.

Lodging at Bath to be near to her business concerning her cargo from Virginia (which has been damaged in a storm), Moll meets an unhappily-married man and after a while, at her own prompting, she becomes his mistress. Six years later, her lover suffers a serious illness, repents of his wrong-doing and returns to his wife. He is generous, looking after their surviving child and settling a good sum on his ex-mistress. Moll makes various investments and one of her trustees falls in love with her, but he is married. Although he is in the process of seeking a divorce, Moll decides against an extra-marital affair and sets off to the north of England in the belief that she will find a wealthy husband there.

In Lancashire, again pretending to be a wealthy widow, Moll meets and marries in a Roman Catholic ceremony a man whom she believes to be a wealthy Irishman. Again, the newly married couple have tricked each other and Moll's 'Lancashire husband', who soon disappears, turns out to be a highwayman. Moll is pregnant, and back in London she gives birth to a boy. Soon, she hears from the trustee of her affairs who had previously fallen in love with her that he has obtained a divorce from his unfaithful wife and wishes to marry Moll. Farming out the highwayman's child, she takes a fifth husband and follows a quiet and domestic life with him and their two children until, after five years, he suffers financial reverses, becomes ill and dies.

Moll is frightened; she is friendless and unaccustomed to the poverty that is staring her in the face. Now forty-eight, she is unlikely to find another admirer to support her; it seems inevitable to her that she must turn to crime. She becomes a skilled thief, her natural ability enhanced by the training given her by a supportive procuress and fence (or dealer in stolen goods) whom she calls 'Mother Midnight'. Unexpectedly, she has a temporary liaison with a baronet whom she robs when he has fallen into a drunken sleep after making love to her. He is foolishly grateful when she returns his property – claiming a reward – and continues to visit her for a time. But Moll's income now depends on her success as a thief, and she becomes notorious although careful to remain as anonymous personally as possible. After a lengthy career in crime and one or two narrow escapes, Moll is – inevitably – captured in possession of stolen goods and committed to Newgate prison. Here she is reunited with her 'Lancashire husband', the highwayman. Moll's repentance earns her a reprieve from the gallows, and she is instead transported, with the highwayman, on a convict ship to Virginia. 'Mother Midnight' buys furniture, food and drink, tools, and general provisions for the couple with some of Moll's savings from her years of crime; on the journey across the Atlantic the couple are well treated by the captain, whom they supply with some of their own food and drink.

Once in Virginia, Moll and her husband are able to buy their freedom and a plantation in Maryland. Her brother, who had been her third husband, is ill, her mother dead. Avoiding a meeting with her brother, she arranges to be reunited with one of her sons, who gives her possession of an inheritance left to her by her mother. Moll and her 'Lancashire husband' live prosperously and happily together, the one-time highwayman able to appear an elegant gentleman. Moll ends her story by explaining that they finally returned to England when she was seventy years old, both sincerely penitent for the sins of their past.

DETAILED SUMMARIES

Defoe did not divide *Moll Flanders* into chapters. For the purpose of these detailed summaries, therefore, his continuous narrative has been divided into sections at various natural breaks in the sequence of Moll's adventures. Page numbers are given for the Penguin Classic edition (see Note on the Text, p. 8).

THE PREFACE (PP. 37–42)

In his role as the transcriber of an autobiography, the author (or the narrator of 'The Preface') explains that this is a 'private History', an account of the life of 'a famous Lady', as received by him in 'a copy'. He has modified the 'Memorandums' somewhat, since the original language was not altogether suitable for the sensitive. His purpose is to make public the history of a criminal life which ended in repentance, in order to present a moral tale.

The author has two main aims in his 'Preface':
- to persuade the reader that this work of fiction is actually a genuine history of the life of Moll Flanders
- to claim that the penitence shown by 'this Lady of Fame' is the 'best and brightest' part of her story of depravity and crime

The reader may well think that the salacious and scandalous details of the life of a prostitute and thief that are offered in the 'Preface' as well as on the title page sit oddly with the narrator's avowed intention to make a moral point.

Newgate the chief London prison of the period

pretends here, claims, professes

modestest Hearer a reminder that literacy was not widespread in the eighteenth century

Gust taste

garbl'd here, pruned, cleansed

be more present to ourselves be more aware of ourselves

the World society

a midwife-keeper here, a brothel keeper

a Child-taker a foster parent, often one who would let a child die from neglect

Voluntier Transport one who agrees voluntarily to exile

SECTION 1 (PP. 43–56)

Early days

Moll knows that she was born in Newgate prison and that her mother, a thief, was transported after escaping hanging. She was apparently looked after for a while by a relative and later wandered with gypsies. Either abandoned by them or having run away, Moll was taken into the care of the parish in Colchester, in Essex, south east England. She stayed until she was fourteen with a kindly woman, whom she calls her 'Nurse', who kept a little school for orphans and foundlings to prepare them for local work as servants. Moll became something of a favourite with her Nurse and with prosperous local ladies and their daughters, who were amused by her desire to become a 'gentlewoman' and gave her sewing work.

When her Nurse died suddenly, the school was closed down. Moll was frightened at the prospect of her impending homelessness. She had only twenty-two shillings which her Nurse had saved for her out of Moll's earnings with her needle and which the Nurse's daughter eventually handed over to the child. Moll was delighted to be rescued from her plight by one of the local ladies, the wife of a prosperous merchant, who took her into the family as a maid and companion to her daughters. Mrs Betty, as she was called at this time, was made much of and shared in the daughters' education in French, music and dancing, by dint of being present at the lessons given at home.

Moll's young life has already taken several changes of direction by the time she is fourteen. Her desire to be a 'gentlewoman', which amuses the local ladies, is, of course, based on a misunderstanding by her of the nature of a gentlewoman of the period. She at first takes it to mean a woman who is not a servant, based on her observation of a local woman – ironically 'a Person of Ill Fame' – who mended and laundered lace. Nevertheless, her desire for gentility persists throughout her life: she marries bigamously and later steals not just to make ends meet, but in order to live like a gentlewoman. At the story's end, she can be said to have succeeded in this aim.

Moll is inclined to give an analysis of her financial assets at various points in the narrative. Here, she mentions the twenty-two shillings which is all that she has in the world when her Nurse's school closes. It is clear that Moll's personality appeals to the local ladies as well as to her Nurse, who had been fond of her, and her life takes a fortunate turn when she is taken in by the prosperous local family.

Old-Bailey the central criminal court in London
the Steps and the String the gallows
an Hospital here, an orphanage
Holland linen from that country
Cheapside a market street in the centre of London
pleaded her Belly appealed for her sentence to be postponed or commuted on the grounds of pregnancy
lac'd Heads lace head-dresses

SECTION 1 continued

> **a meer Mother** here, a real mother
> **huft me** spoke roughly to me

SECTION 2 (PP. 56–102)

Moll in love with one brother, but obliged to marry another

The younger generation of Moll's new family consisted of two brothers as well as the two daughters, with whom Moll spent her time. Moll grew into an attractive young woman and when she was seventeen or so the older son approached her with flattery, protestations of love and promises of marriage. Moll, overwhelmed by his kisses and gifts of money, easily succumbed to his sexual advances. This affair continued clandestinely for some time, unsuspected by the rest of the family. Meanwhile, the younger brother, Robin, had fallen in love with her. The parents were horrified when they discovered that he had proposed marriage to the penniless orphan, and astonished when they found that she had rejected him. The older brother, beginning to tire of his relationship with Moll, saw an escape and bribed her to marry Robin, the family finally making no objections.

The potential discovery on their wedding night that Moll had already lost her virginity was avoided by the older brother making Robin so drunk that he couldn't remember in the morning whether or not he had had sex with her.

Moll passes over in a paragraph or two the five years she spent with Robin before he died; he was a kind husband, but she still loved his brother and was made unhappy by her first lover's continuing presence 'in the country' and then by his marriage to another. Her two children were 'happily' taken in by their grandparents and she tells us that she left with about twelve hundred pounds of her own.

Moll's first love affair with the cynical elder brother seems to cure her of romantic notions about men; although much married subsequently and the mistress of several, she seems never again to have such tender feelings for a man, nor having 'been trick'd once by *that Cheat call'd* LOVE' (p. 103) does she admit to sexual passion again. Her first romance, too, is associated with the money given to her by her seducer: 'I was more confounded with the money, than I was before with the love' (p. 62). The account of the end of her first marriage is accompanied by one of her balance sheets; she mentions her two children, safely disposed of, and the large sum of money she has accumulated as 'a whore to one brother and a wife to the other', as she puts it.

Much of Moll's security in life depends upon discretion and secrecy and this chapter shows her already adept in clandestine matters, as she carries on an affair under the noses of her lover's family.

promising Parts promising abilities

gay here, enjoying a worldly social life

Mrs Betty at this point in the narrative, Moll is known as Mistress Betty, Mistress being the usual polite form of address to adult females and Betty the traditional name for a chambermaid

the Market is against our Sex women are at a disadvantage in the marriage market

all my Spirits flew about my Heart Moll uses the current terminology to explain her emotional state

Capitulation here, stipulation

told the Guineas over counted the money

Correspondence here, communication, intimacy

a Turn-Over a turned down collar, needing a neckcloth to set it off

got vent became known

bred to the Law Robin, unlike his older brother, has a profession

I us'd always to lye with the Eldest Sister beds were often shared and it was unusual for unmarried young women, in particular, to sleep without a female companion

presently immediately

such a rout such a fuss or commotion

what possessions what wild beliefs

Beauty's a Portion beauty serves as a dowry (as well as money)

broke his Mind explained his intention

Rally'd teased

Mrs Mirth-Wit Robin seems to be insulting his sister by a loose reference to a familiar type of comedy actress

Amuse his Sister here, deceive or bemuse his sister

Where Love is the Case,/The Doctor's an Ass a proverbial saying

attack'd her in Form　approached her correctly

says Solomon　a reference to Proverbs 26:4–5

the main Chance　one's own interests, usually financial

like a Bear to the Stake　very reluctantly, like a bear which is tied up in order to be baited (attacked) by dogs

big with the News　full of the news

whether he had had any Conversation with me or no　whether or not he had had sexual intercourse with me

as effectually Criminal　see Matthew 5:28

SECTION 3 (PP. 102–133)

Two more husbands and a journey to Virginia

In London, Moll was in a position to choose a husband from among the acquaintances of her late husband, several of whom made offers of marriage to the prosperous widow. However, the offers came from tradesmen and, although she did not dismiss the idea of marrying a tradesman, she wanted a husband with 'something of a gentleman' about him. Her choice was foolish; her new husband, a draper by trade, was a profligate 'gentleman' and spent her money on high living in two and a quarter years, eventually having to leave London and his wife in a hurry after being arrested and escaping from the 'Bailiff's House'. In order to evade their creditors, Moll had to find lodgings in another part of London and changed her name to Mrs Flanders. Moll's one child of this marriage died.

With her husband in France, Moll felt free to describe herself as a widow again; she managed to salvage some funds from the financial disaster and took refuge for a time in the Mint, a sanctuary for insolvent debtors. Here she came into contact with some members of society's criminal fringe, but did not allow herself to become corrupted. In fact, she made friends with another, genuine widow, who was also aiming to find a new, wealthy husband. When they were able to leave the Mint, Moll went home with her new friend, who gave her some advice about the problems of the 'marriage market'. Moll found a suitable admirer with estates in Virginia and laid a snare for him; they talked of love rather than money, but Moll ensured that he was informed, untruthfully, that she was a wealthy widow. She encouraged this belief by saying that when they were married she would not be prepared to go to Virginia, thereby leaving her suitor to think that she had enough money for them to live in England. Two weeks after the marriage ceremony she admitted that her funds were small; her husband took the news quite cheerfully and they left for Virginia after all.

Moll comes up against the Law in this section when her husband has to run away from his debts, leaving her to undertake various shady activities in order to keep a little money. She encounters criminals in the Mint, where she shelters, and says that she 'was not wicked enough for those Fellows *yet*' – a hint at what is to come.

There is a great deal of discussion about the disadvantaged position of women in the 'marriage market' in this section. Moll agrees with the popular view that men marry only for money; that even a good-looking woman without money has little chance of making a good match unless she employs trickery (see Part Five: Social Background). Moll also claims that men have the upper hand to such an extent that they do not expect ever to be refused, and in fact spread scandalous gossip about any young woman who declines an offer. She exhibits an early example of her well-developed deviousness in a story about how she helped a slighted young woman to get her revenge.

Trepan'd tricked, deceived
a Scarf here, a clergyman's white neck cloth
the Mint a haven, until the early eighteenth century, for those who could not pay their debts
a Spunging-House the bailiffs' place of temporary arrest for debtors
some and some not all at once
pretend to Marry again here, venture to marry again
go quite out of my knowledge go away from where I was known
call'd myself Mrs Flanders the name Moll chose has dubious connotations (see Part Three: Characterisation on Moll)
Lord Rochester's Mistress the reference is to John Wilmot, Earl of Rochester (1648–80), poet and notorious rake, and to a poem of his, warning 'Phyllis' to beware lest she 'Dye with the scandal of a Whore,/And never know the joy'
Redriff now Rotherhithe on the south bank of the Thames

A Woman's ne'er so ruin'd ... a near quotation from Rochester's 'A Letter from Artemisia in the Town to Chloe in the Country'
the Sex women
the occasion of a Character the need for a supportive character reference
Women ought to be the more Nice women ought to be fastidious, particular
as a Horse rushes into the Battle i.e. precipitately
a Lottery state lotteries were approved by Parliament at the beginning of the eighteenth century, and continued until 1824
Cast here, chance, as in cast of the dice
writes upon the Glass of the Sash cuts a message upon the window pane (with his diamond)
I did not care to be Transported I did not want to be exiled – like a convict
shrewdly put to it forced to behave deceitfully
his return of his Plantations his profit from his plantations

SECTION 4 (PP. 133–155)

A terrible discovery

Safely arrived in Virginia, Moll settled happily into married life with her new husband and his mother, 'a mighty chearful good humour'd old lady'. His plantations prospered and Moll learned much about life in her new country from her mother-in-law. The old woman described how the country's labour force arrived as slaves or servants, but were put to work together and eventually were often able to become planters themselves.

After some five years and the birth of two children, and whilst pregnant with a third, Moll learned something from one of the old lady's entertaining stories that horrified her. Her mother-in-law had been describing to Moll how she herself had come over to Virginia as a convicted criminal, showing as evidence the brand burned into the palm of her hand, usually covered by a glove. She had worked hard and had been able to marry her employer after he was widowed; one of their two children was Moll's husband. It was Moll's mother-in-law, after her husband's death, who had built up the plantations into the profitable concern that Moll knew. In part of her story about her early life, the old woman described her arrest and her experiences in Newgate prison. The revelation of her name meant that Moll recognised the old woman as her mother. Moll had married her own half-brother.

Aghast but afraid for three years to reveal the truth, Moll tried to persuade her husband to let her return to England. Relations between them became strained and life unpleasant. Eventually Moll began to hint to her husband what was wrong, and his mother, getting wind of the trouble, persuaded Moll to tell her the terrible facts. The two women decided to keep the secret but finally Moll felt compelled to explain what had happened to her husband. He took it very badly, storming and raging before falling into a state of life-threatening melancholy. It was decided in the family that Moll should leave for England, which she did, leaving the two surviving children behind, and she does not neglect to mention that she 'obtain'd a very good cargo' to take with her.

Moll's adventure abroad and incestuous marriage – illegal in any case, of course, since her second husband is still alive – forms one of the key structural points of this lightly plotted novel, making it possible for the narrative to circle back to Virginia towards the end of the story. Incest in heavyweight literature usually calls for a tragic death or two, but Defoe is out to persuade the reader that this is a 'real life' story; so Moll makes the best of her circumstances, although – recognising her ominous situation – she says that 'all my seeming Prosperity wore off'. Her brother/husband does suffer a fate which acknowledges the literary tradition of doom following even unwitting incest – he lapses into a melancholy state which endures to his death.

Nevertheless, Moll, who has previously weighed up her legal position and found it to her disadvantage, is quite prepared to make a fresh start in England. She takes care to leave with money and a valuable cargo, apparently of tobacco, as well as her brother's promise that he will continue to support her.

froward awkward, obstinate

my Conversation having been unblameable no blame could be attached to my behaviour

the bottom of the thing the truth of the matter

they were equally contemn'd they were equally scorned

a Fit something like an Apoplex a heart attack, possibly, or the first symptoms of his subsequent melancholy

Amasement here, bemusement

Section 4 continued

she fell into her Rhapsodies again she fell into her extravagant expressions again

under your Hand with your signature

Distemper'd in his Head suffering from the madness which is likely to lead to his melancholy

Gotten too great a Head was too far advanced

I felt the Disappointments I suffered the failure of these arrangements

SECTION 5 (PP. 155–182)

A liaison in Bath

On the journey home the ship ran into some rough weather; Moll disembarked in Wales and made her way first to London and then to Bristol, where she eventually found her cargo – and therefore her financial situation – badly damaged. In nearby Bath, 'a Place of Gallantry', Moll guarded her reputation and eventually came under the protection of a man who was unhappily married to a sick wife. Somewhat to Moll's surprise, and even bewilderment, he was prepared to live with Moll without engaging in sexual intercourse. Moll took the opportunity, after they had been drinking one evening, to put a stop to this state of affairs, and they lived together harmoniously as man and wife for six years. After their first child was born (the only one of three to live), Moll's patron took 'handsome Rooms' for her at Hammersmith and Moll entered a period of what she calls 'the height' of her 'Prosperity', although always anxious about her future prospects since she had no legal claim on her lover.

Her fears came true after her lover fell sick. Finding himself 'at the Edge of the Grave', he repented of his sinful relationship with Moll and decided to see her no more, although he sent her fifty pounds and intended to provide for their surviving child. Moll had some savings and extracted a further fifty pounds from her former lover. She hoped for another man to appear who would provide for her, but found 'no encouraging Prospect' and began to fear the future in earnest.

Moll claims to be much troubled in her conscience about her illicit relationship but, as usual, does her best to manipulate events to her advantage. She seems to be anxious to extend her relationship with the patron to include a sexual dimension, since probably she feels that this will give her a greater hold upon him. There is a whiff of blackmail, too, in the means by which she manages to extract a final fifty pounds from him.

Bristol the main English port for ships from the Americas
the Bath a fashionable spa town, so called because of its medicinal waters
the least Reflection the slightest discredit
a wicked Correspondence an immoral relationship
when I was in Bed friends were often received in the bedroom; there is not necessarily any improper suggestion
streighten'd straightened
I must Housewife the money I must conserve, look after, the money
to Dyet him to provide him with meals
Pallate Bed a makeshift bed, probably a straw mattress on the floor
Lady Cleave has connotations of one who would 'cleave', i.e. have illicit sexual relations
in my Travel in my travail, labour in childbirth
Hammersmith at this time, a village to the west of London
by her Relation according to her story
Abroad out of the house
Plate silverware
Painting using cosmetics

SECTION 6 (PP. 183–231)

A proposal and another marriage

Moll, now forty-two years of age, decided to invest her money and live quietly in the country. She met, as one of her trustees, a banker who fell in love with her. He was married to an unfaithful wife and thus his proposal could not be one of marriage, at least until he obtained a divorce. Moll toyed with him, 'as an Angler does with a Trout', to keep his interest in her alive, but decided to try her fortune in the North of England, although she maintained a correspondence with the banker throughout the events that followed. An acquaintance in Moll's lodgings, 'a Gentlewoman', who believed Moll to be a wealthy widow, invited her to Lancashire to meet her family and her brother, a rich man with estates in Ireland, she claimed. Moll was made much of by the Roman Catholic family and, after a whirlwind romance, found herself married, once again, to a man who believed her to have a fortune. Both parties to the marriage were deceived; Moll's 'Lancashire Husband', as she later refers to him, had no estates in Ireland, had spent what he had upon impressing Moll and, moreover, had plotted with a former mistress – who had pretended to be his sister – to entrap Moll.

In spite of all this, Moll and her new husband, Jemy, got on very well together – Moll admits that she 'really loved him most tenderly' – and she even worked out a plan whereby they could make a life together in Virginia. However, they parted in London and Moll found to her dismay that she was pregnant. After making some necessary, discreet arrangements for her 'Lying Inn' with a sinister woman she called 'Mother Midnight', she gave birth to a son, apparently her tenth child.

Moll acknowledges that the latest financial disappointment is caused by the underhand behaviour on both sides in this marriage – 'the deceiv'd Creature that was now my Deceiver' she says of her new husband. Although she seems to have genuine affection for this man, she is prudent enough to keep in touch with the banker, who is courting her by correspondence.

Moll's pregnancy is very inconvenient to her on this occasion, since she has no man to support her through this trying time. She finds anonymity in a raffish part of London and is looked after competently by a woman who seems to be a procuress, a dealer in stolen goods, and an abortionist, as well as a midwife. This dubious character, 'an eminent Lady in her way', provides the lengthy care thought necessary for those giving birth who could afford to pay. Moll gives tariffs for three different grades of care, with full details of the expenses likely to be incurred. (See Part Three: Narrative Mode, for comment on financial detail in the novel, and also Part Five: Social Background, for comments on marriage and divorce.)

Bank Bills, Talleys, Orders Moll prefers silver or gold coin, rather than these pieces of paper

you may Cry her down you may publicly announce you are not responsible for her debts

mend myself improve my financial situation

I would not come too cheap I would not be too easily converted to Roman Catholicism

West-Chester Chester

upon what Foot it was upon what basis, footing, it was

he took a Husbands leave of me he went to sleep

Delamere Forest in Cheshire

to see for a Service to look for work, for a position in a prosperous household

Dunstable a town thirty miles north of London on Watling Street, the old Roman road

a private Lodging in St. John's-street in Clerkenwell, a quarter of north-east London, which had a raffish reputation at this time, and where Moll was able to find anonymity (see the useful 'Maps' section at the end of the Penguin edition)

one of the nicest things in the World a delicate matter, needing fine judgement

Mother Midnight a midwife and/or a procuress, in the language of the street

at the Sign of the Cradle possibly in Cradle Court, near St John's Street

impudent brazen Wench of Drury Lane Breeding insolent girl, probably one of the prostitutes who frequented this theatrical area

clandestinely gotten illegitimately begotten, conceived; a bastard

she would have none got there she would have no children conceived there – i.e. it was not a brothel

an Error of the right Hand an error tending to the right side

another brave Boy another fine boy. This seems to be Moll's tenth child

SECTION 7 (PP. 231–253)

A fifth husband – Moll's 'Friend at the Bank'

Moll was surprised to hear from her correspondent, the banker, that not only had he obtained a divorce from his wife but that she had subsequently killed herself, so that the way was clear for him to renew his offer of marriage in earnest.

Moll's midwife, who had looked after her well, and whom Moll now refers to as her 'Governess', soon persuaded her that she should marry again, arranging for her to board out her latest – and very inconvenient – child, to a poor woman. Moll did arrange visiting rights on this occasion, commenting belatedly on the duties of a mother.

Moll's long postponed meeting with her admirer took place at an inn on the London to Chester road at 'Brickill', Moll having to keep up the pretence that she had been all this time in the north of England. After many shy protestations, Moll married her banker in a ceremony of dubious legality.

The honeymoon in the inn was interrupted by an incident which disturbed Moll. Looking out of the window one day, Moll saw three men go into an inn opposite to the one where she was staying. Not only was one her 'Lancashire Husband', but they were subsequently revealed to be highwaymen, when a 'Hue and Cry' was set up after them. Moll at first had been frightened that her former husband had come after her in anger; after they had ridden off, and she realised that she was safe, she spoke up as a witness to the good character of one of the three men, hoping to help her highwayman husband.

Moll relished the comforts of an easy life with her banker husband, had two more children and even 'wept over the Remembrance of past Follies'. This quiet and contented life came to an end after five years: the shock of the loss of money through the bankruptcy of a partner caused her industrious husband to fall ill and he soon died, leaving Moll with little to support her.

Moll's 'Governess' is one of a series of women, sometimes criminally inclined, whom she presents as guides. However, although she makes good use of what her Governess can offer in the way of practical help and advice, Moll is careful, as always, to maintain secrecy about most of her past. As to the future, Moll lets the woman believe that she is to be married to a husband who lives in the north, and is, at this stage in her life, 'well satisfied to have been freed from such a House' as that of Mother Midnight.

The reappearance of Moll's 'Lancashire Husband', which reveals that he is highwayman, is a moment of high drama. Moll's first thought is for herself; when she is satisfied that she is not at risk, she is good-natured enough to do what service she can for her former husband. As one of the few characters to reappear in this episodic novel, the incident also serves a purpose in terms of the plot.

a contriv'd Method for Murther an apparently legal means of disposing of unwanted children (by letting them die of neglect)

all Vapours all due to a dizziness, faintness or depression

Hertford about twenty miles north of London – a likely place for farming out unwanted children

This puzzl'd me scurvily this was a sore problem

Stone in Cheshire Moll is vague; Stone is in Staffordshire

Stoney Stratford ... Brickill coaching halts on the London to Chester road

Non Compos Mentis Latin: not in control of one's mind; insane

Chagreen shagreen – a rough leather, often dyed green

the Consent of Friends here, the consent of responsible relatives or guardians

not tyed by the Canons to Marry no where but in the Church not obliged by Canon Law to marry in church – although a licence was needed to marry elsewhere

it was all Grimace it was all put on, pretence

a good Suit of Knots a good set of ribbon bows

Bone-lace for a Head lace (made on fine bone bobbins) for a head-dress

a great clutter a great commotion

a Hue and Cry the clamorous pursuit of a suspected criminal

the Mob Gentry those comprising the crowd pursuing the highwaymen – here, 'Gentry' is an ironically polite term

Covetousness is the Root of all Evil see 1 Timothy 6:10

till I come to the Experiment until I can discuss it from experience

to keep an Equipage to own a coach and horses, and to keep its necessary attendants

Lethargick morbidly apathetic, listless

SECTION 8 (PP. 252–292)

'Give me not Poverty lest I steal'

Moll found herself in a frightening situation. She managed to live for three years on what little money she had, exchanging her house for lodgings and selling some of her belongings.

Scared and fearing real deprivation, Moll turned to crime. She took the opportunity to snatch an unwatched bundle of linen and other goods from an apothecary's shop and successfully made off with it. She was terrified of the possible consequences – she had committed a capital crime – and remorseful 'for three or four Days time'. She continued to find tempting opportunities; in the next recorded incident, she came across a child going home alone from dancing school who was wearing a necklace of gold beads. Moll took the child into a dark alley and removed the necklace without its knowledge. She admitted that she was tempted to murder the child, but put this idea from her. She justified this crime to herself by claiming that the incident would warn the parents not to let the child wander on its own.

Moll continued to have 'a great many Adventures', including one in which she was the opportunist beneficiary of another thief's crime, and another involving the theft of two rings from a shelf inside the window of a house.

Moll needed a fence, someone who could help her to sell her booty for a good price, and rediscovered Mother Midnight. Her 'Governess' was not as prosperous as she had been, but was now a pawnbroker, amongst other things, and was thus able to assist Moll. Moll learned that, although she had not been able to pay for the support of her son by the highwayman in the last few years, he was well, and Mother Midnight arranged for her remaining child by her last husband to be boarded out as well. (One had presumably died.) Moll moved into the woman's house, coming to an understanding as to what Moll's trade really was. Soon Mother Midnight was arranging lessons in pickpocketing for Moll. Moll became very skilled at this and persisted with her life of crime even after her instructress was arrested and executed. Moll tried working with accomplices, but found it too dangerous, and in one partnership which involved masculine disguise she only just managed to evade capture after her partner betrayed her, since he described her as a man. She was relieved, however, to hear 'the joyful News that he was hang'd'.

In spite of the many arrests of her acquaintances, Moll persisted in her opportunist thefts, although she had managed to save enough money to live upon. As always, she was cautious and secretive in her dealings with others; although her name, Moll Flanders, became widely known, she ensured that her identity was unclear and her address unknown to others.

Moll is anxious to justify her recourse to theft. She offers many statements showing that she believes that poverty is to be dreaded as 'the worst of all snares' and almost inevitably will lead to crime. She fears being caught, and displays remorse on many occasions. Nevertheless, 'as Poverty brought me to the Mire,' she says, 'So Avarice kept me in'. (Defoe himself, twice bankrupted, was very conscious of the effects of poverty, or the fear of it. See Part Five: Daniel Defoe's Life.) Moll is obviously proud of her skills, and offers a varied selection of crimes in which her proficiency is demonstrated. Above all, she is an imaginative opportunist, seizing her chances as they arise. She soon becomes hardened to the wretched fates of others, putting her own safety first.

The accurate detail Moll gives of the London of her time is one of the aspects of realism that gives authenticity to the novel.

Leadenhall-street one of the main shop-lined streets in the City of London
Billinsgate Billingsgate was, until 1982, London's fish market beside the Thames
Bartholomew Close ... Holbourn-bridge a detailed account of Moll's route (see the Maps section at the end of the Penguin edition)
one who stood up one who stood out of the way (of the crowd)
several Peices of Silk separate, different pieces of silk
fain to sell it pleased or obliged, to sell it
good Prizes good prices
this necessary Woman this useful woman
helped me to Spark helped me to find a suitor
into the Box frankly into the small room, booth, openly
Moll Cutpurse a real and notorious seventeenth-century pickpocket and cutter of the strings by which purses were attached, usually to the waist
snap'd by a Hawks-ey'd Journeyman caught by a keen-eyed, experienced employee
voted Quick with Child declared to be pregnant
burying Rings rings bought as mementoes of a dead benefactor
no Gust no taste, inclination
a scouring a severe examination, a beating – or, here, a hanging
Flanders-Lace the importation of Flanders lace was prohibited; much prized, it was often smuggled into England

he began to Capitulate with me he began to bargain, come to an agreement, with me

I very punctually divided this Spoil I very punctiliously divided the booty

the Rage of the Street mob violence, which could result in the death of its victims

a Key to the Clue a key to the clew, the elaborate combination, the tangle

Shop-Keepers Comptors shop counters

to discover his Accomplices to reveal, betray, his accomplices

a formal story here, a detailed story

to clear myself off to get rid of the stolen damask

to run a Tick to keep the score, a list – of the thefts she had resumed

SECTION 9 (PP. 292–307)

The Baronet at Bartholomew Fair

By this time over fifty years of age, Moll was surprised by the attentions of 'a Gentleman extreamly well Dress'd'. She was at Bartholomew Fair, assessing the possibilities of finding some opportunity to follow her thieving trade, when she was approached by a man who clearly found her attractive. She accompanied him for the rest of the evening, during which he became very drunk and finally went to bed with Moll. In the coach in the early hours of the morning, he fell asleep and Moll took the opportunity to steal his money, his periwig, his sword and various other portable items, slipping out of the coach at a convenient moment. With the help of her Governess, Moll was subsequently able to sell back his belongings to this unfortunate man, a baronet; he was delighted to recover his property and to be reassured that he had not been in danger of infection from syphilis. Recognising that his secret was safe from his wife, he continued occasional sexual encounters for a year or so; he did not make Moll rich, but was generous enough to free her from the need to follow her 'old Trade' for a while.

> In this episode, Moll can be seen very clearly as able to exploit even unexpected possibilities. She indulges, as usual, in a great deal of moralising – not only about her own misdeeds, but about those of the foolish baronet and the risks he was running by picking up someone like herself. Moll says that she 'was not so past the Merry part of Life, as to forget how to behave' when a man

wanted to make love to her, and obviously relishes this 'unlook'd for' adventure.

It is Moll's Governess who evolves an elaborate plan with a trusted 'Friend' to persuade the baronet to buy back his belongings, and who eventually enables the sexual encounters to continue. Moll is, of course, a willing accomplice in all these arrangements.

Bartholomew Fair an anciently established fair, held in Smithfield, London, for two weeks from the saint's day (24 August). Ben Jonson's play, *Bartholomew Fair*, 1614, shows that it was already a disreputable annual event.

the Cloisters the covered walk in front of shops and booths

Spring-Garden, at Knight's-Bridge pleasure gardens of unsavoury reputation

a Dart strikes through their Liver (see Proverbs 7:22–3)

the foul Disease syphilis

guilded Counters fake gold coins

what she should officiously propose what she would obligingly propose

I do not come to make a Booty of you I don't intend to blackmail you

this was his Grievance this was his worry

Chair-man man who, with another, carries a sedan chair

tho' he did not Keep though he did not provide for Moll on a regular basis

SECTION 10 (PP. 308–349)

Moll is finally brought to justice

Her liaison with the baronet over, Moll resumed her successful career as a skilful and ingenious thief, sometimes disguised as a poor woman 'in a very mean Habit', sometimes dressed to show various degrees of prosperity. In spite of her caution, however, she began to be a recognisable figure, at least amongst the criminal fraternity.

On one occasion, she was detained as a thief, but charged with a theft she had not committed. She balanced the opportunity to make money on a charge of wrongful arrest with her need to keep out of the public eye and, with the assistance of a helpful lawyer, decided to press for a settlement out of court. She won not only high compensation of £150, but also received a 'Suit of black silk Cloaths' and payment for her legal charges, as well as apologies and a good supper.

Moll was 'the richest of the Trade in England' but could not persuade herself to give up her life of crime. Audacious and an ever more skilful thief, she enjoyed many profitable adventures and some narrow escapes. She managed to talk herself out of being charged with the intention of stealing some silver from an empty shop, mainly because she was well dressed and had plenty of money with her. Just three days after this incident, 'not at all made Cautious' by this incident, she was caught in the act of escaping with two pieces of brocaded silk from what seemed to be a private house.

She was almost successful in her pleas for mercy, but the law took its course and she found herself in Newgate prison, the dreaded place, she says, 'that had so long expected me, and which with so much Art and Success I had so long avoided'.

Moll's pride in her successful career as a thief is ever more evident. It is clear that she enjoys the excitement and thrill of her criminal adventures, which she continues in spite of having amassed enough money to support herself. A sense of the inevitability of Moll's eventual downfall is created throughout the account of her criminal life. Many accomplices and criminal acquaintances are captured, and often hanged; although Moll has several narrow escapes and eludes justice by her quick thinking and acting ability, Newgate always beckons.

I had several Shapes I had several disguises; here, Moll dresses as a servant
Barnet, Toteridge ... Hadley at that time, north of London on the main coaching road to Scotland
Stratford and Bow at that time, still villages
if he had the Marks of it if he had the identifying name or number
Flint Glasses from Mr. Henzill's Glass-house good quality glasses (made from ground flint) from a well-known manufacturer of glass in Newcastle upon Tyne
when does the Pitcher come safe home that goes so often to the Well a relevant variation of a proverb relating to the inevitable end of all things (see Ecclesiastes 12:6)
a Constable the duty of preserving the peace fell upon local householders, appointed annually by the parish officers. Hired substitutes (notoriously corrupt) took the place of those who avoided their duty by payment of a fine

second Mourning a widow's mourning clothes for the first year after the death of her husband were of unrelieved black; 'second mourning' clothes were less rigorously gloomy, perhaps with trimmings

Hick's Hall ... the Old Bailey criminal courts

a petty Fogging hedge Soliciter an inferior lawyer; the implication of 'hedge' solicitor is that he is not to be found at a regular address

I abated his Cringes I cut short his abject apologies

in such a Plight here, in such a wretched attire

publick Notice would be given in the Gazette the loss would be advertised in the government journal, *The London Gazette*

any I ever sorted with any I ever consorted with

burnt to Death at a Stake the punishment for counterfeiters of coins; Moll puns on the word 'Dye', the forger's mould

a Paper of Lace a parcel of lace

the Mall at that time, a place where the fashionable took the air

the Horse-Guards cavalry parade grounds beside St James's Park

I would have told them I would have counted them

Tunbridge and Epsom after Bath, the most fashionable spa towns of the day

an old Bite a well-established trick

some Purchase here, some gain

Wash-balls soap

the honest Clown the naïve rustic

scratching his Pole scratching his head (poll)

the fatal Tree the gallows

SECTION **11** (PP. 348–394)

Repentance and a reprieve

Moll was a notorious criminal who had been long awaited at Newgate; her fellow prisoners met her with a mixture of mockery and encouragement, traditionally drinking her health in brandy – at her expense.

In spite of all the efforts of her devoted friend Mother Midnight to subvert the course of justice, Moll was eventually brought to trial and sentenced to death. She recognised that her first penitence – when she arrived at Newgate – had been worthless, since her regrets were only that she had been caught. Now, facing death, she was brought to genuine repentance for her sinful life by a minister sent to her by the grief-stricken Mother Midnight, who had herself repented of her former life. The minister, impressed by Moll's sincerity, was able to have her sentence commuted from death to transportation.

Meanwhile, Moll had been astonished to witness the arrival at Newgate, three months before her reprieve, of her 'Lancashire husband', Jemy the highwayman. With the time of his trial approaching, she visited him. There was a fond reunion and Moll persuaded him to accept transportation if, as expected, it was offered him, although he claimed that he would have preferred death to the dishonour, as he saw it, of 'Servitude and hard Labour'.

After various obstacles were overcome and much plotting and planning, Moll was joined on board ship by the reluctant Jemy. She had high hopes for their future in Virginia, since her trusted friend and Governess, Mother Midnight, had managed to send her on board valuables, linens, clothes and other goods, as well as hidden money to start a new life in the country with which Moll was already familiar.

The sincerity of Moll's repentance (as well as of her habitual moralising) has caused much controversy in critical discussions of the novel (see Part Six: Critical History). The degree of **irony** in the novel detected by the reader is likely to be a key factor in a decision on this matter.

Defoe himself was bankrupt and imprisoned for debt on several occasions and this personal experience of the horrors and humiliation of life in jail gives real authenticity to the account of Moll's months in prison, although conditions in the debtors' prisons (the Fleet and the King's Bench) were not quite as dreadful as those in Newgate, in which he spent only a short space of time.

my Score my bill – prisoners had to pay for their food and drink
the College slang for Newgate – suggesting perhaps that inmates improved their criminal skills by learning from each other in prison
I shall hear the Bell ring Defoe's own note assumes that the ordinary reader will not understand this reference to the execution bell
The Ordinary of Newgate the prison chaplain

to nauseate the Man to find the man intolerable

at Guild-Hall at the seat of the Corporation of the City of London

were pursu'd by the Country were pursued by the people of those parts

these brave topping Gentlemen these elegantly dressed, gallant men (highwaymen were known as 'gentlemen' of the road)

remov'd into the Press-Yard moved into the better accommodation offered by a part of the prison which had to be paid for

buy a Horse and take a Tour take to the road on horseback and become a highwayman

Hind, or Whitney, or the Golden Farmer three notorious seventeenth-century highwaymen. All were executed

My Temper was touch'd my feelings were affected

finding the Bill finding a case to be answered; a preliminary to actual trial

as white as a Clout as white as a sheet (clout=cloth)

made their impudent Mocks upon that made fun of that

Bedlam from 'Bethlehem', the London hospital where the mentally ill could be viewed by the paying public as an entertainment

of meer Course naturally

the Recorder one of Moll's judges

a severe Satyr a heavy satire, a serious misreading

a meer Distemper an utter collapse

he would not have me secure he did not want me to believe myself safe

the Master's side one of the part of Newgate where conditions were worst

Hockly Hockliffe in Bedfordshire

Burford Fair Burford is in Oxfordshire

parted too hardly with their Money would not give up their money without a fight

with any Temper here, with an even temper, dispassionately

kept in Hold kept in custody

the Ship weigh'd, and fell down the River the ship raised its anchor and set off downstream

a little better Furniture some better belongings

drag'd along with three Keepers pulled along by three prison warders (Jemy's pride is hurt by this treatment)

SECTION 12 (PP. 394–427)

Moll's final years

Moll's Governess, Mother Midnight, continued in her efforts to secure the future in the Americas for her protegée and Jemy. She arranged with the captain of the convict ship for necessary furniture and tools for plantation life to be taken on board, and discovered from him how the couple could buy their freedom on arrival. Provisions in the form of food and drink were used to 'treat our benefactor, the captain' and Moll and her highwayman husband enjoyed a comfortable voyage to their new life.

On arrival in Virginia, the captain organised a little legal juggling which resulted in freedom for Moll and Jemy. Finding her mother to be dead, but her third husband – her brother – to be still alive, Moll decided to move away and buy a plantation further afield; circumstances found them settling in Maryland. Within a year they had had a timber house built, tobacco planted to sell and crops established for their own needs.

Moll, however, was constantly wondering about 'the grand Affair of what my Mother had done for me' and whether the promised legacy was waiting for her in Virginia. Finally, she made herself known to her son, who lived with his invalid father; he was very welcoming and readily arranged to pay her the income from the plantation which her mother had left her. She did not meet her former husband/brother again and, conveniently, he soon died, so that Moll was able to clear up with her husband the mysteries about her past, and to introduce her son to him as though they were only recently married.

The eight years in Maryland were happy and prosperous, Jemy blessing the day he married Moll in Lancashire. When they returned to England, Moll was seventy years old, they were both 'in good Heart and Health' and intent on spending their last years in – no doubt comfortable – 'Penitence for the wicked Lives' they had lived.

> So, with the support of the faithful Governess and the judicious employment of her own ill-gotten gains, Moll's sentence of transportation offers instead of punishment the opportunity for a new and prosperous life as a plantation owner.
>
> Her marital complications are reasonably well resolved; she is reunited with the son she somewhat strangely refers to as her 'one

and only child'; her mother has left her a legacy and Jemy, enjoying the life of a leisured gentleman, is able to work out that their assets total 'a very good Fortune'.

Moll is triumphant at their material success, and it is not until the final lines of her narrative, now back in England, that she mentions spiritual matters; the reader is likely to wonder what form the penitence of this comfortably placed old couple will take.

he return'd presently he replied immediately, not 'later', as in modern usage

the Steerage an open part of the quarter deck; Moll perhaps chooses an informal cabin in this accommodation rather than in that of the superior 'great Cabbin' because she needs the space for her many boxes. In any case, Moll is very privileged in comparison to the other convicts, who pass the voyage imprisoned below deck in the hold

his round House the captain's quarters

Gravesend a point down Thames where ships were cleared by the customs before the voyage out

the largest River in Ireland the Shannon

his Freighter the contractor for a cargo – in this case, convicts who would be sold in the Colonies

as I have related at Large as I have related fully, at length

a Chairwoman a charwoman, daily domestic servant

any other Country any other region

Night-Flyers prisoners who, with the connivance of corrupt warders, were freed at night to follow their trade as thieves

Thief-Catchers government informers, who often were double dealers who worked with thieves as well

not only unacquainted, but indolent Jemy was not only unused to work, but had the gentlemanly habit of laziness too

Writings of Gift legal deeds, assigning the ownership of the plantation to Moll

Land enough cur'd enough virgin land prepared for planting

a Meeting-House in London probably a dissenters' place of worship

Yatch yacht

giving her part sharing with her

PART THREE

CRITICAL APPROACHES

CHARACTERISATION

A look at the characterisation in a novel is probably the readiest means to a first critical approach. In Defoe's novel, Moll's presence is overwhelming to an extent unusual even in a fictional autobiography such as this. All the events and encounters with other characters are received via Moll's consciousness only; it is her **viewpoint** that dominates, as she shares her thoughts with us, counts her money and values her goods, moralises and gives her usually self-flattering accounts of her fortunes and misfortunes. So, although a few other characters – those respected by Moll – merit attention, it is the nature of Moll herself, the interpreter of her own life, which demands critical attention. The comments below, therefore, are a beginning to an analysis of Defoe's presentation of Moll – an analysis which will continue throughout the various aspects of much of what follows in this Note.

MOLL

A LIFE OF MIXED FORTUNES

Moll's is a life of sharp changes of fortune right from the beginning: born in squalor in Newgate, she is fortunate after a perilous infancy to be taken in by a decent woman, her 'Nurse', who brings her up carefully and affectionately. Unfortunate that her substitute mother dies and homelessness looms, she is lucky enough to be taken in by a prosperous family. Unfortunately, her seducer, the elder son of the household, does not marry her. Fortunately, his younger brother does. This kind of sequence sets the pattern for Moll's life, which continues with spells of prosperity alternating with the fear of destitution; her life takes a darker turn when she becomes a thief, successful for many years, but inevitably caught at last. The clouds of this deepest misfortune soon lift, however, and Moll ends her life a wealthy woman, and claiming to be a penitent one.

Facing the downturns in her fortunes, Moll is never the passive heroine, but takes what action she can, given the limits of her circumstances. While she still has her looks she exploits the men who are attracted to her; when she is past 'the merry part of Life' (p. 294) she pits her wits and skill against conventional society as a thief.

A 'GENTLEWOMAN'

Even as a child, being trained by her Nurse in housework, Moll rejects the idea of going into service. She has a horror of becoming 'a Drudge to some Cook-Maid' (p. 46) and takes as her model a local woman, who is not a servant but who mends and washes lace; Moll describes her as a 'Gentlewoman', not knowing that she is in fact 'a Person of ill Fame' (p. 51) with several illegitimate children. This mistake, as her Nurse fears, foreshadows Moll's own future situation.

Moll's aspiration to be a gentlewoman is one that persists throughout the story of her life. Often, she can lay claim to this status by virtue of her husband's position. Widowed by the death of her first husband, a lawyer, she believes that she will marry a 'Tradesman', but looks for one 'that was something of a Gentleman too' (p. 104). She enjoys the brief spell that follows as they spend her legacy and savings in a year of would-be aristocratic high life, but finally regrets the marriage to 'this Land-water-thing call'd, a Gentleman-Tradesman' (p. 104). In her subsequent marriages and liaisons, she tries to ensure that she is forming an alliance with a prosperous gentleman, although sometimes she is duped.

Even in her spell as a thief, she can refer to herself as a gentlewoman. For example, when she is attempting to steal a purse in a crowd at a chapel or Dissenters' place of worship, she refers to her intended victim as 'tother Gentlewoman' (p. 277).

Transported as a felon, she is nevertheless recognised as a gentlewoman by the captain and boatswain (p. 395) on the convict ship. These two examples of course relate to Moll's style of dress in the first case and to her obvious possession of means in the second. In other words, gentility needs to be backed by money in Moll's world. Like her mother, once a convict, later 'the old Gentlewoman', Moll ends her life as the owner of plantations in the Colonies, and therefore is able to fulfil her childhood desire, when she would 'Cry all Day' (p. 47)

at the prospect of going into service and wanted instead to be a
gentlewoman.

MOLL'S HUSBANDS AND LOVERS

As Moll grows up, she is soon well aware of the potential of her personal
charms to improve her lot in life, and exploits these assets whilst they last,
usually in a calculated way. Nevertheless, she has several spells of calm
contentment in her life with men who love her, sometimes 'to
Distraction', as she claims. She does not dwell upon these respites in a
turbulent life, as lacking in interest to the reader; it is worth remembering
this ability to live affectionately, or at least contentedly, with men whom
she has accepted for their status as financial support. In other words, she
makes what could be seen as a fair return to some of the men whom,
otherwise, she would seem to be cynically exploiting.

Moll was clearly already an attractive young woman when she
joined the merchant's household in Colchester. She was, she says, 'taken
for very Handsome, or if you please for a great Beauty' (p. 56). She had
the character, too, she believed, 'of a very sober, modest, and virtuous
young Woman' (p. 57). The older son of the house sets about seducing
her with flattery, promises of marriage, kisses and gold, and she easily
succumbs to his advances, demonstrating early the discretion – which
always stands her in good stead – necessary to keep the affair secret. Moll
is in love with her seducer but likes his money as much as his advances:
'I was more confounded with the Money than I was with the Love'
(p. 62), she says, and she counted 'the Guineas over and over a thousand
times a Day' (p. 64). It is only too likely that Moll would find this dashing
and persuasive young man irresistible, and only too likely, as well, that he
would soon tire of her after his cynical seduction. His betrayal of her
makes her seriously ill, not only because she loved him 'to Distraction' but
because, she says, of 'the loss of all the Expectations I had' of marriage
(p. 83).

The younger son, Robin, is also attracted to Moll, but his intentions
are honourable. The older brother, glad to escape from a now wearying
entanglement, helps Robin to persuade their parents to agree to the
match. Moll passes over her five years of marriage to this worthy young
man in a paragraph, admitting that he was as 'tender, kind good-
humour'd Man as any Woman could desire' (p. 102). But she had been

unable to forget her first lover and, bitter as she was at his disloyalty, she 'never was in Bed with my Husband, but I wish'd my self in the Arms of his Brother' (p. 102).

Moll's choice of a next husband is a poor one. She marries a financially reckless 'Gentleman-Tradesman'; he spends her money as well as his own like water and, although she enjoys a brief, extravagant lifestyle, living 'like Quality' (p. 106), disaster soon strikes. Her husband, badly in debt, disappears to France; Moll has to decamp, too, moving her lodgings and changing her name. Moll shows no resentment towards her husband; just as she accepted that she was a willing partner in her affair with her first lover, so she admits that she enjoyed sharing the experience of living like members of the spendthrift aristocracy. So far as the loss of her own money went, she 'had some of the spending it too' (p. 105).

Moll, presenting herself as a widow again, even though she has a living husband, needs to find a new husband who will support her. After much plotting with a shrewd friend, she is able to trick an American planter into marriage with her. She does not possess the fortune she had caused him to believe was hers, but he takes this well and they settle comfortably in Virginia with Moll's mother-in-law. 'I thought myself the happiest Creature alive,' she says (p. 133), until she discovers that she has made an incestuous marriage. This is one occasion when she is ultimately unable to quiet her conscience in the interests of financial security; she feels she must give up her life with her brother. She returns to England, leaving him melancholic and 'a little Distemper'd in his Head' (p. 154), a state from which he never recovers.

Not destitute, but again looking for a man to support her, back in England Moll becomes the protegée of a wealthy man. Moll's landlady in Bath describes him as 'a Man of Honour and of Virtue' and, more importantly perhaps, 'of a great Estate' (p. 160). Moll says that 'his Company was very agreeable to me' (p. 159) and again she settles into a contented life, looking after him when he is ill and persuading him to make her his mistress. When, after a serious illness, he decides to give up this unlawful relationship, Moll is concerned to get as much money from him as she can.

Looking for a more stable relationship again, Moll (with two living husbands as far as she knows) presents herself again as a wealthy widow. After a whirlwind courtship, she once more tricks a man into marrying her; this time, she is tricked, too, when it appears that her 'Lancashire husband' is penniless, having spent what he had in a grand show of wealth in order to capture her. After the mutual discovery of false pretences, they try ruefully to make the best of things. Moll is in love with 'J.E.' – James, or Jemy, as she calls him. 'I would have gone with him thro' the World, if I had beg'd my Bread' (p. 210), she says, but Jemy disappears, to reappear as a highwayman and, eventually, as Moll's last partner. He retains his glamour for her, even in Newgate, it seems. She relishes the fact that he is a gentleman and even feels it to be her fault that he has to become a highwayman after his disappointment in her as a wealthy woman. Towards the end of Moll's narrative, in the colonies, she recognises that 'I lov'd my Lancashire husband entirely, as indeed I had ever done from the beginning' (p. 419) and she is delighted to be able to make what she sees as reparation to him, by providing him with all the material trappings of a gentleman, and seeing him live the leisured life of a gentleman planter.

But, meanwhile, Moll has married for a fifth time, to a banker who had previously made advances to her, but whom she had rejected as he had a wife living. His unfaithful wife divorced and dead, Moll prepares to marry him, although she has one of her frequent fits of remorse:

> … what an abominable Creature am I! And how is this innocent Gentleman
> going to be abus'd by me! How little does he think, that having Divorc'd a Whore,
> he is throwing himself into the Arms of another! that he is going to Marry one
> that has lain with two Brothers, and has had three Children by her own Brother!
> one that was born in *Newgate*, whose Mother was a Whore, and is now a
> transported Thief; one that has lain with thirteen Men, and has had a Child since
> he saw me! (p. 243–4)

Here she sums up her history of relationships with men at the age of around forty. She has told us about her two lovers and four husbands so far; that leaves seven of the 'thirteen Men' she mentions unaccounted for. This seems to be explained in the 'Preface', where the reader is told that 'some of the vicious part of her Life, which could not be modestly told, is quite left out' (p. 38).

When, after eight years of the 'utmost Tranquility' (p. 251), Moll is left almost destitute, she is too old to find another prosperous husband, or even to 'Spark' as she puts it. She does have one more lover about whom she tells us, however – a drunken nobleman whom she robs after going to bed with him. She despises him for being 'a Fop so blinded by his Appetite' that he 'should not know an old Woman from a young' (p. 294) but later, when he wishes to continue the liaison, she amiably falls in with his inclinations. However, it is clear, as she has already recognised, that her days of real sexual allure are over; her lover visits only occasionally and, although generous, does not offer to keep her on a settled income.

MOLL AS MOTHER

Moll apparently has twelve children. Five of them die, we understand – this would not be unusual in a time of high infant mortality – and the other seven are soon disposed of by Moll, who can certainly not be described as a devoted mother. We hear little else of any of them but one. Of her living children, the two of her first marriage are left with their grandparents; of her incestuous marriage, the two who survive out of the three born in Virginia are left there with their father and grandmother; the upbringing of her child by her reformed lover (one of three surviving) is undertaken by him; her son by the highwayman is farmed out and paid for, at least for a while, by Moll; and the surviving child of the two from her final marriage soon disappears from the narrative.

It is the son she left in Virginia whom she meets again when he is an adult. Moll describes what she sees as a touching meeting with the man she refers to surprisingly as 'her one, and only Child' (p. 416). There are many tears and kisses; she gives him a fine gold watch, adding 'I did not indeed tell him that I had stole it from a Gentlewomans side, at a Meeting-House in London, that's by the way' (p. 422). He gives her the deeds to the plantation left to her by her mother, which he was to manage for her, and a bag of gold representing the current year's profits. This exchange of kisses and gold towards the end of Moll's life may remind the reader of the similar exchange between herself and her first lover, in the family of the merchant who took in Moll as a young woman (see below, Language and Style, for further comment upon this apparent echo).

CRIME AND PENITENCE

If Moll often expresses remorse at the 'Wickedness' of her sexual adventures, her life of crime brings even more moralising. A memorable pattern is created in her narrative of triumphant boasting about her many and varied exploits, interspersed with a commentary including occasional bouts of what she claims is disgust and horror at her activities. There must be many opportunities for successful crime for 'one so exquisitely keen in the Trade' (p. 343), as her Governess describes her, and Moll takes them with relish, claiming to be 'the greatest Artist of my time,' who worked herself 'out of every Danger with such Dexterity ... tho' many times in the extreamest Danger' (p. 280). She is honest enough to recognise, however, that she always failed to be really penitent about her crimes. Even her misery when she is finally taken to Newgate prison is not a sincere rejection of her crimes, because, she says, 'all my Repentance appear'd to me to be only the Effect of my fear of Death, not a sincere regret for the wicked Life that I had liv'd' (p. 353). She does claim to be a true penitent when wealth and a happy life with Jemy, the highwayman, have brought her to the age of seventy; in the last sentence of the narrative, Moll says 'we resolve to spend the Remainder of our Years in sincere Penitence, for the wicked Lives we have lived.' The degree to which the reader accepts Moll as a genuine penitent is likely to vary. Some see her as a brazen old reprobate, others accept that her penitence is real, or at least that she herself is persuaded of her own sincerity. (See Part Six: Critical History, for more comment on this crucial matter.)

MOLL'S NAME

The reader never learns the real name, or names, of the much-married woman who becomes notorious as Moll Flanders. There are some ordinary explanations for this. One of them is that fictional characters were often not fully named, or were represented by pseudonyms, or as 'Mr ——', or as on p. 220 of *Moll Flanders*, where Mother Midnight is introduced as 'Mrs. B ——', as were real people in scandal sheets and gossip columns of the day. This could help Defoe in his intention to make the reader believe in Moll as a real life character. But, more to the point, Moll is a secretive character who does not let the different aspects of her life overlap. She does not reveal the full names of any of her husbands, at least partly because most of her marriages are illegal and she does not want her husbands or lovers to know anything of each other. A name that she assumes, and reveals to the reader, when she gives birth to the absent Bath lover's son, is the deliberately bawdy one of 'Lady Cleave', implying a wanton woman, apparently a joke acknowledging her unconventional situation (p. 169).

Discreet as a wife or mistress, she has to be equally circumspect as a thief, not identifying her occasional accomplices in theft, nor giving her real name to any of them. 'Moll Flanders' is a name widely known by the time she goes to Newgate prison, but Moll takes care to remain a shadowy figure and it is not a name which could have had a face put to it until she meets her fellow criminals in jail.

The name that Defoe's heroine chooses to be known by is (like the temporary 'Lady Cleave') an obvious signal to the reader of the nature of her character. She spends her early years with the merchant's family in Colchester as 'Mrs Betty', the traditional name for a chambermaid, and probably one not much to Moll's liking, given her dreams of gentility. There is perhaps a hint of her rejection of this name with its connotations of servitude when she says, as she leaves her children with her dead husband's parents, 'and that by the way was all they got by Mrs Betty' (p. 102).

It is when she has to escape her second husband's creditors that she takes a lodging in the Mint: 'in a very private Place,' she says, 'drest me up in the Habit of a Widow, and call'd myself Mrs Flanders' (p. 108). As commentators have pointed out, 'Flanders' has immediate associations not only with lace – Moll's early preoccupation, and often later the target of her thieving expeditions – but more significantly with prostitution. From the sixteenth until well into the nineteenth century, London brothels were known for their Dutch or Flanders prostitutes.

There was considerable trade with Flanders (e.g. bricks, horses, wagons) although the importation of Flanders lace was illegal, in order to protect the British trade. Although Flanders lace was of high quality, 'Flanders' could be a derogatory term: a dictionary of thieves' cant by 'B.E.', published in 1700 and likely to have been known to Defoe, defines 'Flanders-fortunes' as being 'of small Substance' and 'Flanders pieces' as 'Pictures that look fair at a distance, but coarser near at Hand'. Both of these references strike home when related to Moll.

Her nickname, Moll, itself has seedy connotations. At Newgate, she describes how she was first Mrs Mary Flanders, then Mrs Molly Flanders and after that descended to 'plain Moll Flanders' (p. 350). The most obvious reference is to a real and notorious late sixteenth to early seventeenth-century thief, known as Moll Cut-Purse. A sympathetic version of that Moll featured in Middleton's and Dekker's comic drama, *The Roaring Girl, or Moll Cut-Purse* (1611). 'Moll', too, has long had connotations, particularly in thieves' slang, of a prostitute or of the accomplice or female companion of a male criminal.

So the heroine of Defoe's story is known to the reader by the name which cannot be disassociated from her criminal activities and which seems to flaunt this dramatic aspect of her life. However, it does appear that a change of name accompanies her penitence in the narrative's final part. In the Americas, the setting for her spiritual development (as well as for her great worldly prosperity), she resumes her 'real Name' (p. 393), as the reader learns when Moll has her goods forwarded to her in Virginia under the name that she has never revealed, but which can perhaps be assumed to represent the 'real' Moll.

OTHER CHARACTERS

Although she is a secretive and sometimes lonely figure, Moll's life often takes her into a busy world. The reader is aware of the bustle in the inns on the roads that she travels, of packed pleasure gardens and, particularly, of the liveliness of the London streets, where Moll spends most of her years as a thief. A crowd is often invoked: sometimes, for instance, the throng leaving a Meeting-House provides the skilled pickpocket with the chance to practise her trade; or the crowd gathered at a house fire offers anonymity and the opportunity to carry away someone else's goods under the pretext of helping. Sometimes it is a frightening mob, like that which set off on the 'Hue and Cry' after Moll's highwayman husband, or the mob which offered rough justice to a thief caught red-handed in the street.

However, in spite of living in a densely populated world for much of her life, Moll dominates the narrative; other characters remain shadowy, being, of course, known only through her interpretation. But several characters merit further scrutiny.

JEMY THE HIGHWAYMAN

Most of her husbands and lovers, mentioned under 'Moll', above, are seen as foils to the central character, to be exploited and offering the opportunity for her to quote flattering views of herself. Jemy, however, or James, is rather different from the others. At first, of course, believing him to be wealthy, Moll tricks him into marriage, looking for the economic advantage she seeks from men. Each the dupe of the other, they make the best of the double confidence trick and find themselves in love. Moll weeps bitterly when Jemy, penniless, has to leave her. She blames herself for his returning to highway robbery as a livelihood; when they meet again in Newgate prison and it appears that they have the opportunity of a new life in the Americas, she is the economic provider from her considerable savings. She very much enjoys the role of generous, wealthy wife, and her lifelong dream of gentility is realised by the fact that her husband is a gentleman, albeit one who has turned to crime. She seems almost proud of the fact that because he was 'bred a Gentleman', he was 'not only unacquainted, but indolent' (p. 411), meaning that his upbringing had left him unwilling and even unable to work on their plantation.

Her highwayman lover adds a touch of low-life glamour to her story, since the highwayman was a figure of romance and admiration – at least in folk myth. 'The Preface' offers a brief reference to Jemy who, it seems' 'liv'd a twelve Years Life of successful Villany upon the Road, and even at last came off so well, as to be a Voluntier Transport, not a Convict; and in whose Life there is an incredible Variety' (p. 42). Moll's account of Jemy's life as told to her in prison (p. 384) describes Jemy rather differently as having 'carried on that desperate Trade full five and Twenty Year'. Some idea of the reckless, dashing nature of the highwayman's life also appears: '… the Success he had met with, had been so very uncommon, and such, that sometimes he had liv'd handsomely and retir'd, in one Place for a Year or two at a time, keeping himself and a Man-Servant to wait on him, and has often sat in the Coffee-Houses, and heard the very People who he had robb'd give Accounts of their being robb'd, and of the Places and Circumstances, so that he cou'd easily remember that it was the same' (p. 384). The perils and physical dangers of such a life are also outlined on p. 379, when he shows Moll the scars of the severe wounds he has received from swords and pistols. The highwayman's glamorous apogee came probably a little later than the publication of *Moll Flanders* (1722) with Gay's popular musical play *'The Beggar's Opera'* (1728); the romantic image of the mounted 'Gentleman of the Road' of course bore little relation to the reality of violent crime. Highwaymen took open risks by challenging coaches, which usually had armed men or guards aboard.

MOLL'S MENTORS

Except for the duration of her final years with Jemy, and of her spells as a married or kept woman, Moll usually has a female adviser or friend in the background. Her Nurse, as she calls her, who brings her up in the charity school, is a decent, honest woman. Moll describes her as 'a very sober pious Woman' and lists her other qualities as '(2.) Very Housewifly and Clean, and (3.) Very Mannerly, and with good Behaviour' (p. 46). She pays tribute to her Nurse's training later, when she is disguised as a poor and dirty beggar for one of her thief's outings: 'I naturally abhorr'd Dirt and Rags; I had been bred up Tite and Cleanly, and could be no other, what ever Condition I was in' (p. 325). Moll is fortunate in this kindly woman, who, she says, brings up the girls in her care 'as Mannerly and as Genteely as if we had been at the Dancing School' (p. 46). The reader guesses that Moll's attractive personality is already at work in her early years, since she clearly charms her Nurse, who makes something of a pet of her.

Moll's mother-in-law, whom she recognises as her own mother in Virginia, is her confidante in the problems of the incestuous marriage she has made with her half-brother. Her life foreshadows that of Moll in that she faced death in Newgate for the theft of some cloth and had her sentence mitigated to transportation. She lives a long life in Virginia, able to put the past behind her and to enjoy such prosperity that she is able eventually to leave a useful legacy to Moll. Moll's mother's story and her own experience of life in Virginia enable her to make optimistic plans for a new life there when she is transported. But her mother's conscience is even less troubled than that of Moll. She recommends carrying on as though nothing had happened after Moll learns that she is married to her own brother: for, she says, 'we are both undone if it comes out' (p. 146).

If Moll's own mother is unable to act as a satisfactory moral guide, then her Governess is a mentor many degrees more cynical. Moll first encounters her as 'Mrs B ——' or 'Mother Midnight', when she needs to give birth discreetly to the highwayman's child. Moll's admiration of the excellent arrangements made by the midwife – 'she was an eminent Lady in her way' (p. 225) – is tempered by her repugnance for the extent of the woman's activities; she is a procuress and abortionist as well as an experienced midwife. Even more abhorrently, her 'wicked Practice' was to find means of disposing of 'Women's unwelcome Burthen of a Child clandestinely gotten' (p. 227). She finds a satisfactory 'Cottager's Wife' to take over Moll's own child, however, and Moll is alternately grateful to her and horrified by her, as is shown by the various epithets she uses to describe her at this stage in the narrative. Often by now referred to as 'my Governess', as well as 'the old Woman' and 'the old Beldam', she begins to address her as 'Mother'; but when she departs (typically setting a false trail), expecting to marry her fifth husband, she says her goodbyes, 'well satisfied to have been freed from such a House, however good my Accommodations there had been' (p. 239).

Soon, of course, Moll is back. After the death of her last husband and some experiments in crime, she realises she needs a fence, someone who will buy stolen goods from her. She returns to her Governess, now 'not in such flourishing Circumstances as before' (p. 261), but having added pawn-broking to her legitimate trades. This practised rogue is Moll's adviser and support throughout her years of successful criminal exploits and is an invaluable friend when Moll is finally caught. She it is who tries to interfere with witnesses against Moll and who, when bribes and other means have failed and Moll is to be transported, makes sure that she is well equipped for her life abroad. She remains faithful to the end, sending Moll's savings to her in Maryland. The tale of her extraordinary life of crime, which ends as do those of Moll and Jemy in penitence, is referred to in Defoe's 'Preface' alongside that of Jemy as needing volumes of its own for it to be told. There is no doubt that the Governess profits from Moll's skill as a thief, but her affection and loyalty go beyond what her protegée's money-making prowess might justify. This relationship, bearing witness to the traditional concept of 'honour among thieves', serves, too, to show the universal attractiveness of Moll's personality; she is as much a favourite of her wicked Governess as she was of her honest Nurse of early years.

Defoe is often identified as the writer of fiction who first used fully realised settings for his work, and this is especially true of *Moll Flanders* with its vivid depiction of the life of the period. If a case is to be made out for Defoe as our first major novelist, the claim must include the citing of the detailed **realism** which he introduced into fiction, the development of which in its many aspects was a crucial part of the development of the novel itself. Further comments on Defoe's role in the advance of techniques of the novel may be found in Part Six: Critical History.

If Defoe's characters, apart from Moll herself, are shadowy, this is certainly not true of his settings in *Moll Flanders*, which often provide the reader with details which make streets, buildings, rooms and their contents come alive. This is undoubtedly the case in the descriptions of settings during Moll's extended period as a thief, usually in London. The routes she takes through the narrow congested city streets, often doubling back or turning into even smaller side ways or alleys to evade pursuit, may be followed on a map of the period, as in the early episode of the theft of a gold necklace from a child (pp. 257–8). Soon after this exploit Moll steals a silver tankard from a tavern (pp. 263–4) and the reader gets a picture of the layout of the building: '... when going by an Alehouse I saw the Door of a little room open, next the very Street, and on the Table a silver Tankard ... I went into the Box frankly ...'. She orders 'a pint of warm Ale', and hears the serving boy go down to the cellar to fetch it, and she hears the 'Woman in the Bar' ask about the tankard in 'the Five', indicating that there are at least four other 'Boxes' or rooms.

Of course, the focus in this scene is the valuable gleaming tankard, which Moll manages to carry away safely. The details, too, that she gives of the contents of shops are all related to their value and to her intention to get hold of them: gold and silver goods, heaps and pieces of linen, damask, silk and – particularly – lace are described and often later priced, and the reader is aware of the busy commercial life of the city and of the constant vigilance needed by the traders to keep thieving hands off their wares.

By means of clever confidence tricks, Moll manages the opportunist theft of several bundles of personal belongings, and even of a large box. As she gloats over the value of the contents, the modern reader is given a glimpse of the valued possessions of the day. One bundle, stolen from a flustered servant girl, contained clothes, lace and linen (p. 310);

another, carried away by Moll under pretence of assisting at a house fire (pp. 271–2) contained the family valuables – silver, a gold watch, rings and gold coins, amongst other things. One of her most outrageous thefts gave her a consignment of goods sent from a warehouse at Newcastle upon Tyne, 'the Box being full of Linnen, and the Hamper full of Glass-Ware' (p. 310).

Like Defoe himself, Moll often has occasion to travel, and there is much evidence of the arduous nature of the journeys on the roads of the day and of the inns at which Moll stayed, arriving by coach, on horseback or, when secrecy required it, taking 'a Passage in a Waggon' (p. 342). An appreciation of the beauty of nature and the countryside would be unexpected at this period and is not present; Moll has a typical city-dweller's belief that rural folk are more likely to be easily exploited, and makes fun of one 'honest Clown' who scratches his 'Pole' (poll = head) for a long time before he is able to answer her question (p. 341).

Some detail is given at the end of the narrative of country life in the Americas. Moll and her highwayman husband, making a new and better life, are appropriately enough developing a plantation out of virgin soil. Within a year in Maryland they 'had near fifty Acres of Land clear'd, part of it enclos'd, and some of it Planted with Tobacco, tho' not much; besides, we had Garden ground, and Corn sufficient to help supply our Servants with Roots, and Herbs, and Bread' (pp. 414–5). The cargo sent out to Moll by her Governess gives a picture of their life: Moll is delighted to give her husband the accoutrements of a gentleman – wigs, swords, guns, a fine saddle and a scarlet cloak; there are also clothes and linen, 'Iron-Work of all sorts, Harness for Horses, Tools, Cloaths for Servants, and Woollen-Cloth, stuffs, Serges, Stockings, Shoes, Hats and the like, such as Servants wear' (p. 425). Three 'lusty Wenches' arrive with the cargo, to add to their workers, one of them fortunately pregnant and thus soon bringing an additional 'stout Boy' to work for Moll. (See note on servants and slaves in Part Five: Social Background.) On one of the final pages, Moll offers the successful balance-sheet that the new life has brought her: almost incredulously joyful, Jemy counts out on his fingers the considerable sum of their possessions. A little earlier in the narrative, exclaiming at his good fortune, he had said, 'What is God a doing for such an ungrateful Dog as I am!' (p. 423) and the reader is perhaps inclined to agree that penitence and a new life have brought a wonderful prosperity to the erstwhile criminals.

NARRATIVE MODE

Defoe makes two claims for the mode of presentation of Moll's life – that she wrote her account at the end of her life, and that he has moderated her language and omitted the most shocking incidents.

Moll, then, is supposed to be giving an account of her history from the viewpoint of serene old age, a story of which she has in large part already disburdened herself to the Minister in Newgate: 'I gave him the Picture of my Conduct for 50 Years in Miniature' (p. 366). And yet, apart from a good deal of moralising, her narrative demonstrates little or none of the detached and mellow judgement that old age might be expected to bring. Her accounts of vital moments in her life are as urgent as if they had happened yesterday, and Moll comes sharply into focus when she is recounting exciting meetings with her first lover, for instance, or giving triumphant descriptions of her daring and successful thefts. Thus, although Defoe makes the gesture of claiming that this story has been twice told by an ageing Moll, and modified by himself, what the reader needs, and often gets, is an account told by Moll with striking immediacy.

In this first person narrative, it is her account of the events that make up her life that gives a forward movement to her story (See Time and Structure below). Moll gives her history in a variety of narrative modes: sometimes in a brisk account of external events; sometimes through an account of her somewhat shaky logical thinking (in, for instance, planning and justifying her many crimes); and often in a reconstruction of her emotions when facing loss, destitution or criminal trial, when sometimes remorse bites deep. The first person narrative often includes **reported speech**, as well as some telling **direct speech**, sometimes extending to quite lengthy dramatic scenes, in which Moll of course comes off well. There are several such scenes in Moll's early years, when she is involved with both brothers at the merchant's house in Chichester. At least two of these (pp. 84–5 and 87–9) occur downstairs when she is upstairs ill in bed, and Robin's flattering remarks about Moll and witty exchanges with his jealous sisters are rather mysteriously reconstructed by Moll ('I heard of it', she offers as an explanation on p. 85).

Other exchanges also show Moll's defensive and manipulative skills in scenes of extended dialogue, as in her verbal fencing with the wealthy banker, married at the time to 'a Whore' but to be her fifth husband (pp. 189–92).

Some incidents, then, are re-created in vivid scenes, with plenty of dialogue to enhance verisimilitude. Her emotions are dealt with in a more sombre fashion. Her several happy spells of married life are briefly passed over, but her grief and distress are examined in detail when she finds herself without the protection of a husband and faced with poverty, and later, when she fears for her life as a result of the capture of accomplices, and after her own arrest. When she first comes up against the prospect of real destitution, after the death of her fifth husband, she weeps incessantly – as she had when she was a little girl faced with the life of a domestic servant, and when her highwayman husband left her. The account of excessive grief, which lasted for two years, begins to turn into one of Moll's many moralising passages – often offering a justification of what she is about to do, or has just done. 'Give me not Poverty lest I Steal', she misquotes from the Bible (p. 254), a theme which is often returned to in the story of Moll's crimes. Poverty does, in fact, drive her to her first theft (pp. 254–5) and to an emotional mixture of horror, excitement, confusion and short-lived remorse (pp. 255–6), expressed in something which begins to approach an 'imitation of the mind's experience', as Virginia Woolf described her developments in the **stream of consciousness** some two hundred years later.

The moralising that follows links her, as so often, with the writer of 'The Preface', who claims to have tidied up the tale and who feels it necessary to announce to the reader that *Moll Flanders* is an improving work. It is in the frequent moralising passages, particularly those expressing penitence, or would-be penitence, that Moll's identity seems to merge with that of the writer of 'The Preface'. For example, the moralising at various points about the dangers of that 'Poverty which is the sure Bane of Virtue' (p. 250), 'the worst of all Snares' (p. 251) – to give two of many examples – was a particular preoccupation of Defoe himself, financially unstable throughout his life (see Part Five: Daniel

Defoe's Life). Defoe, the author of the work, has of course created the character of Moll, and her narrative; has he also created the writer of 'The Preface', or was he writing as Daniel Defoe, journalist and novelist? The original version was published anonymously, no doubt to preserve the pretence of authenticity, but the writer of the immensely popular *Robinson Crusoe* (1719) was likely to be soon identified. It is usually assumed that the writer of 'The Preface' may be taken to be Defoe himself; it is a point which merits discussion because if this is the case then the charges of hypocrisy often levelled at Moll may also be levelled at Defoe as represented in his 'Preface'. If it is not the case, and Moll's editor is an invented character, then it is the degree of **irony** which is present in the work which is a major question, rather than the degree of hypocrisy. This knotty problem is further discussed in Part Six: Critical History.

It can be shown that the apparently simple narrative structure of *Moll Flanders* is in fact more complicated than it at first appears (see also Time and Structure below). Nevertheless, the effect created by Defoe is in the end straightforward enough; Moll is able to tell her tale – a self-serving and one-sided account, it is true – and it is the diary-like immediacy of the narrative that comes to the fore.

TIME & STRUCTURE

Often described as episodic or **picaresque** (see Language and Style below), *Moll Flanders* is a work of fiction which has little formal plot, but which relies for its effect upon a sequence of separate incidents linked by the constant presence of the narrator herself.

Such plot as there is relates to Moll's journeys to the Americas. Her first trip to Virginia (during her incestuous marriage) involves a meeting with her long-lost convict mother and makes her familiar with plantation life and its potential for a genteel prosperity. Her second trip abroad (after transportation as a convict herself), with her highwayman husband, finds them soon settling into a comfortable life as planters; her mother has left her a legacy; her incestuous brother dies, leaving her with probably only one husband. They return to England eventually, aged and wealthy. The two dislocations from England to the American colonies may be said, during the first visit, to offer the discovery of a new country and, in the second, the chance to exploit its possibilities. (See Part Six: Recent Criticism for further comment.) Moll makes it clear that these possibilities involve the accumulation of considerable wealth for those who have a little capital and, of course, she claims that in a new country her life takes on a new spiritual dimension with the recognition of the need for penitence.

Otherwise, the structure of the novel is chronological, with Moll's life related as it might be in an occasional journal, focusing on what Moll sees as the highlights and disasters of her marriages and liaisons and of her criminal career – and with a **closure** that finds her prosperous and apparently at peace with her conscience.

This life span, from childhood to old age, forms a natural structure, and the reader is hardly aware of some of the time anomalies involved. As discussed in Narrative Mode, above, although the story is presented with the immediacy of incidents which have happened recently – on the day of recording even – the author claims that it is the reconstructed history of an old woman of seventy. It is a twice-told tale, too, since she rehearsed most of it to the Minister in the prison in a kind of confession. *Moll Flanders* was published in 1722, but the author pretends that Moll's 'Memorandums' were 'Written in the Year 1683' (p. 427). She was born, then, around 1613, in the reign of James I. She would therefore have lived through the reign of Charles I, and the English Civil War which preceded the king's execution, and through the Protectorate of Oliver Cromwell, and would have been alive through most of the reign of Charles II, after the restoration of the monarchy in 1660. These were stirring times which included religious persecution and martyrdoms, plague and the Great Fire, and wars abroad as well as at home. No mention of these momentous national events filters through into her narrative, and there is little to suggest that Moll lives in the seventeenth rather than the eighteenth century; the details of her everyday life point to the sense that Moll was actually living in a period closer to that of her first readers' experience than the given date claims, just as Hogarth's portrait of Moll reproduced on the cover of the Penguin Classic edition shows her in eighteenth rather than seventeenth-century dress. Another work of fiction published by Defoe in the same year as *Moll Flanders* also claimed to be a true story and was also set back in the seventeenth century. *A Journal of the Plague Year* recorded the frightening events of 1665 when the plague in London was at its height, and convinced most readers that it was an eye-witness account. Defoe would have been about five years old at the time, but doubtless had access later to evidence from those who had experienced this horrible epidemic. The removal of a narrative from time and space is a well-known device to aid belief in its veracity; the date of 1665 was historically necessary in the case of *The Journal of the Plague Year*. In the case of *Moll Flanders*, however, it seems that Defoe gave his heroine a date of birth set ninety years in the past in order to support his claims that hers was a true story. It also made her a near contemporary of the notorious and popular seventeenth-century thief, Moll Cut-Purse, on whom Moll Flanders is partly modelled.

LANGUAGE & STYLE

In a literary period when elegance and wit were highly prized, and constant classical references assumed the reader to have shared the writer's formal education, Defoe's blunt and naturalistic style clearly does not belong to the mainstream of admired writers (see Part Five: Literary Background, for further comment on Defoe's standing with his contemporaries).

In his own time, Defoe was best known as a journalist, and there is no doubt that his style owes more to his experience in this profession than to the grand literature of his period. In fact, the personal voice of Defoe's prose style in, for instance, *The Review* – which he published between 1704 and 1713 and often wrote single-handed – is consistent with that he employs in *Moll Flanders*. As a journalist, he explained to the readers of his *Review* that he intended to write with 'a down-right plainness' such as would appeal to a wider readership more than merely to an élite. By the elevated literary standards of the day his style seems rough and ready, but he intentionally avoided anything too demanding of the reader's abilities. Then, too, he achieved a prodigious output in the year that saw *Moll Flanders* published – over three thousand pages, according to Ian Watt in *The Rise of the Novel* (p. 103). This offers some explanation for the lack of polish of his writing generally and for some inconsistencies in the narrative.

Thus, one of the formative elements of his inelegant style is his journalistic background and his desire to reach a wide readership. Another is his familiarity with the **rogue biographies** of the day, popular and realistic accounts of the lives of criminals. It is to these narratives, with their factual backgrounds and social authenticity, that the events of *Moll Flanders* relate, rather than to the **picaresque** tradition. Both **genres** are episodic in form, but the picaresque belongs entirely to a comic tradition, in which trickery and jokes predominate. Plausibility is often second to ingenuity in these anecdotal narratives. Watt (ibid, p. 111) points out that *Moll Flanders* approaches closest the picaresque in the least convincing of her escapades, such as the double confidence trick played upon each other by Moll and her Lancashire husband, or the damages for false arrest that Moll gets from the mercer who arrested her. In any case, Defoe valued the truth and **realism** which he believed could be found in biographies and life, rather than in fiction; his own novels are always written, with the aim of achieving authenticity, in an autobiographical form.

Although an everyday realism is achieved, Moll lives in a narrow world. As mentioned in Time and Structure, above, none of the many major events of history is allowed to penetrate her consciousness. Nor does she ever apparently read a book, although we know that she has learned to play and sing. However, not altogether convincingly, she shows a certain literary wit in the episode (pp. 125–6) where she joins in a **stichomythic** exercise with her husband/brother as he professes his love and she her cynicism in a poetic exchange scratched upon a window pane. This is one of the very few acknowledgements of literary devices by Defoe in a narrative which is itself notable for its lack of such enhancements.

If, however, there are no classical references in Defoe's narrative, such as eighteenth-century readers were used to finding, there are several biblical ones, usually adapted. Moll draws on Proverbs 30:8–9 in the New Testament, for instance, in her expression of fear at what poverty might bring her to: 'Give me not Poverty lest I Steal', and there are several other examples, usually variations on this theme, drawn from the Bible.

There is little imagery in Moll's speech, except for a few unexceptional examples in common currency: e.g., 'that terrible Bug-bear going to Service' (p. 50); 'and so laid down the Cudgels' (p. 126), when her husband/brother admits defeat in their poetic encounter on the window pane, as mentioned above; 'since it was come to that pitch' (p. 201); 'took a Husband's leave' (p. 209), i.e. went to sleep; 'the fatal Tree' (p. 348), i.e. the gallows. And, of course, Moll – who seems to see life as a balance-sheet – often uses the language of commerce when she is speaking of marriage: she refers to the 'market' in this connection more than once, as for instance on p. 112: '… the Market run very Unhappily on the Mens side', referring to what she and her friend see as a situation that favours men in marriage choices. The last words she records by Jemy show him praising her for having turned out to offer him a financial reward after all: 'I think I have married a Fortune, and a very good Fortune, too' (p. 426).

The horrors of her incarceration in Newgate bring Moll to use some rather more striking language: she describes the morally numbing effect of association with hardened criminals in a simile as being 'like the Waters in the Cavities, and Hollows of Mountains, which petrifies and turns into Stone whatever they are suffer'd to drop upon …' (p. 354). The experience of prison, too, brings her to describe the place in terms of imagery: '… the hellish Noise, the Roaring, Swearing and Clamour, the Stench and Nastiness, and all the dreadful croud (crowd) of Afflicting things that I saw there; joyn'd together to make the place seem an **emblem** of Hell itself, and a kind of Entrance into it.' (p. 349). Otherwise, **symbolism** is hard to find, although it is possible, of course, to see the whole tale as symbolic of the human journey through life, with sin and repentance its key Christian features, and with Defoe's fellow Dissenter, John Bunyan, offering an earlier model in *The Pilgrim's Progress* (1678–84) (see Part Five: Background, for an outline of Defoe as Dissenter).

If, in general, Defoe makes little use of decorative devices in *Moll Flanders*, there is one feature of his work which is rather unusual, and that is his use of parallel incidents, or near repetitions of events. For instance:

- Moll wants as a child to be a 'Gentlewoman', and takes as her model a woman who in fact is 'a Person of ill Fame' – a situation which she replicates in her life
- The lace which provides part of the means of support of this supposed gentlewoman features large in Moll's career as a thief, and is connected to her name (see Moll's Name above, under Moll in Characterisation)

- What she sees as the incestuous marriage she makes with the younger brother of her first lover is echoed in the reality of her genuinely incestuous marriage to her half brother
- When she goes to the Americas – and finally makes her fortune – Moll is repeating part of the story of her mother's life
- Moll gives accounts on more than one occasion of adventures relating to gold watches: one of her first successful thefts was that of a gold watch from a young woman, heavily pregnant, who was leaving church (p. 266). A second, unsuccessful attempt, also had as intended victim a woman at a religious 'Meeting House' (p. 277), and a third involved the valuables, including a gold watch, which Moll stole from a drunken lover (p. 293). She takes a gold watch from her pretended acquaintance, Lady Betty, in the Mall, as they see the King go by (p. 331) and another from a slightly drunken lady in 'a little Country *Opera*-House' (p. 337). Towards the end of her narrative, the now supposedly penitent Moll thinks it appropriate to give one of two gold watches in her possession to her rediscovered Virginian son: this, too, was a watch stolen from 'a Gentlewoman's Side, at a Meeting-House in London' (p. 422)

T̲EXTUAL ANALYSIS

TEXT 1 (PP. 104–6)

For the first time in her life, Moll is in charge of her own fortunes. Having lost her first love and been married for five years to his brother – a good husband, but one for whom she had no feeling – she is now an attractive young widow, her children provided for and herself in possession of a small fortune of twelve hundred pounds. She enjoys life and society with her friend, a linen draper's sister, is courted by many 'very considerable Tradesmen' but makes her own choice of a new husband:

> Well, at last I found this amphibious Creature, this *Landwater-thing* call'd, *a Gentleman-Tradesman*; and as a just Plague upon my Folly, I was catch'd in the very Snare, which *as I might say*, I laid for my self; *I say laid for my self*, for I was not Trepan'd I confess, but I betray'd my self.

> This was a *Draper* too, for tho' my Comrade would have brought me to a Bargain with her Brother, yet when it came to the Point, it was it seems for a Mistress, not a Wife, and I kept true to this Notion, that a Woman should never be kept for a Mistress, that had Money to keep her self.

> Thus my Pride, not my Principle, my Money, not my Virtue, kept me Honest; tho' as it prov'd, I found I had much better have been Sold by my *She Comrade* to her Brother, than have Sold my self as I did to a Tradesman that was Rake, Gentleman, Shop keeper, and Beggar all together.

> But I was hurried on (by my Fancy to a Gentleman) to Ruin my self in the grossest Manner that ever Woman did; for my new Husband coming to a lump of Money at once, fell into such a profusion of Expence, that all I had, and all he had before, if he had any thing worth mentioning, would not have held it out above one Year.

> He was very fond of me for about a quarter of a Year, and what I got by that, was, that I had the pleasure of seeing a great deal of my Money spent upon my self, and as I may say, had some of the spending it too: Come my dear, *says he to me one Day*, Shall we go and take a turn into the Country for about a Week? Ay, my

Dear, *says I*, Whither would you go? I care not whither *says he*, but I have a
mind to look like Quality for a Week; we'll go to OXFORD *says he*: How *says I*,
shall we go, I am no Horse Woman, and 'tis too far for a Coach; too far *says he*, no
Place is too far for a Coach and Six: If I carry you out, you shall Travel like a
Dutchess; hum *says I*, my Dear 'tis a Frolick, but if you have a mind to it I don't
care. Well the time was appointed, we had a rich Coach, very good Horses, a
Coachman, Postilion, and two Footmen in very good Liveries; a Gentleman on
Horseback, and a Page with a Feather in his Hat upon another Horse; The
Servants all call'd him my Lord, and the Inn-Keepers you may be sure did the like,
and I was *her Honour*, the Countess; and thus we Travel'd to OXFORD, and a
very pleasant Journey we had; for, give him his due, not a Beggar alive knew better
how to be a Lord than my Husband: We saw all the Rareties at OXFORD, talk'd
with two or three Fellows of Colleges, about putting out a young Nephew, that
was left to his Lordship's Care, to the University, and of their being his Tutors;
we diverted our selves with bantering several other poor Scholars, with hopes of
being at least his Lordship's Chaplains and putting on a Scarf; and thus having
liv'd like Quality indeed, as to Expence, we went away for *Northampton*, and in a
word, in about twelve Days ramble came Home again, to the Tune of about
93 *l.* Expence.

Vanity is the perfection of a Fop; my Husband had this Excellence, that he valued
nothing of Expence, and as his History you may be sure, has very little weight in
it; 'tis enough to tell you, that in about two Years and a Quarter he Broke, and was
not so happy to get over into the *Mint*, but got into a *Spunging-House*, being
Arrested in an Action too heavy for him to give Bail to, so he sent for me to come
to him.

Moll is a lively, somewhat wilful and reckless young woman at this stage
in her life. As usual, supposedly re-telling her tale from the wisdom of old
age, she moralises at length about events, but her vivid account at the
heart of this episode about the extravagant jaunt to Oxford is what is
memorable in this extract.

Moll ruefully confesses that she brought the disaster of her second
marriage upon herself by her enduring desire to lay a claim to gentility.
She believes, with hindsight, that the notion of a 'Gentleman-
Tradesman' is a contradictory one, and that she might have done better
to accept the draper brother of her friend rather than this 'Landwater-
thing' her new husband, who, although a draper himself, affected the

style of a gentleman, at a time when class distinction meant that such a combination was uneasy, or even impossible.

As she often does, Moll makes some rather conflicting statements about her moral position. She would not become her friend's brother's mistress, she claims, because she believed that she should marry or, if she had money enough, support herself, rather than become a kept woman. She admits that it was her pride and her money that kept her 'Honest', rather than principle and virtue; nevertheless she abandons any claim to an ethical stance when she follows this with the material judgement that, after all, she would have been better off as the friend's brother's mistress than as the wife of her spendthrift husband.

Moll's account of their short life together, in which her new husband spent all her money as well as whatever he had – 'a great Deal' of it on Moll – shows that she enjoyed the extravagance of it all. In the early days of the marriage – 'he was very fond of me for about a quarter of a Year' – Moll enjoyed the fun and extravagance; her description of the twelve day 'ramble' to Oxford and Northampton in a coach with six horses and all the trappings of nobility demonstrates her keen delight in the 'Frolick'. This instance of recklessness leads on to her account of her husband's inevitable financial ruin, from which Moll distances herself after clearly having gone along whole-heartedly with the earlier Oxford exploit.

We learn later that her husband escapes to France, doing what little he can for Moll, and plays no further part in her story.

The measured style of Moll the moralist, which introduces and ends this extract, is strikingly different from the rapid pace of her account of the Oxford 'Frolick'. It has sometimes been observed that in the more penitent passages the style of the narrative seems to echo that of 'The Preface'. It is a surprise, for instance, to find Moll in possession of the term 'amphibious', although her translation into 'this *Landwater-thing*' rings true. 'A just Plague upon my Folly', 'catch'd in the very Snare', with their biblical overtones, have an echo of Defoe the Dissenter (see Part Five: Background). The weighty literary **balance** of '… my Pride, not my Principle, my Money, not my Virtue, kept me Honest …' sounds more like Defoe the journalist than the voice which the author gives to Moll. That voice is, however, very distinct in the core of this extract, where the words tumble over each other in the headiness of her account of the

Oxford adventure. Here is a young couple out for the kind of good time which involves 'a profusion of Expence' upon themselves and a bit of fun at the expense of others. As the adventure is planned, Moll moves, as she occasionally does, into **direct speech**, unfamiliarly set out in continuous prose. Moll easily falls in with her reckless husband's plan. Although her 'hum *says* I' carries all the weight of wifely concern, this is soon abandoned as she adds 'my Dear 'tis a Frolick, but if you have a mind to it I don't care.' In fact, not only did she not 'care', but she actually revelled in the grandeur of the expedition, as she describes their elaborate equipage: the coach, with its 'very good' horses, and their retinue of temporary servants – five men, plus 'a Page with Feather in his Hat upon another Horse', a detail which helps to bring it all to life. Pretending to be a lord (an earl, perhaps) and his countess, they travel in great style, enjoying the Oxford 'Rareties', apparently convincing several academics of their credentials and leading on their victims to believe that the supposed aristocrats are in a position to employ them as tutors to an imaginary nephew. They enjoy further unkind teasing when 'bantering' some 'poor Scholars', giving them hopes of employment as clergy to the impostors. The full stops are few in the description of the coach tour and the **syntax** is informal, giving an immediacy that is typical of Moll at the height of her story-telling. This particular tale she is telling against herself, of course, admitting her willing complicity in the disastrous extravagance. Before and after the account of the expensive outing, however, she distances herself from blame, as she usually does. She makes a biting comment, too, about her husband, during the story of the Oxford masquerade: 'not a Beggar alive knew better how to be a Lord than my Husband,' recognising the reality of the inevitable ruin which lay ahead and seeing her husband already as a beggar rather than the 'Quality' whose style he was aping.

It is no surprise to find many references to 'Money', spending and 'Expence' in this passage, since they are relevant to the incident. The inclusion of an actual sum – 93*l.* – is typical, too, of Moll's realistic details. The extravagance results, appropriately, in the husband's bankruptcy, his failure as a debtor to get into the relative security of the Mint, and his imprisonment in a bailiff's 'Spunging-House', followed later by his escape from his creditors (see Part Five: Daniel Defoe's Life, for the author's own financial troubles). But the language of the marketplace extends, as so often in the narrative, to less financially-sensitive passages: Moll speaks here, at the beginning of the extract, of being brought 'to a Bargain' with her friend's brother, and of being 'Sold' by her friend or 'Sold' by herself. Her 'Ruin' in the earlier part of her story related to her loss of virginity to her first lover; now she says 'I was hurried on (by my Fancy to a Gentleman) to Ruin myself in the grossest Manner that ever Woman did' – this time, of course, the 'Ruin' relates to money.

TEXT 2   (PP. 257–8)

Moll's fear of poverty has driven her to her first crime, the theft of a bundle belonging to a customer at an apothecary's shop. Frightened and repentant for 'three or four days', she soon feels the 'wicked Impulse' again to 'go out and seek for what might happen':

> I went out now by Day-light, and wandred about I knew not whither, and in search of I knew not what, when the Devil put a Snare in my way of a dreadful Nature indeed, and such a one as I have never had before or since; going thro' *Aldersgate-street* there was a pretty little Child had been at a Dancing-School, and was going home, all alone, and my Prompter, like a true Devil, set me upon this innocent Creature; I talk'd to it, and it prattl'd to me again, and I took it by the Hand and led it a long till I came to a pav'd Alley that goes into *Bartholomew Close*, and I led it in there; the Child said that was not its way home; I said, yes, my Dear it is, I'll show you the way home; the Child had a little Necklace on of Gold Beads, and I had my Eye upon that, and in the dark of the Alley I stoop'd, pretending to mend the Child's Clog that was loose, and took off her Necklace and the Child never felt it, and so led the Child on again: Here, I say, the Devil put me upon killing the Child in the dark Alley, that it might not Cry; but the very thought frighted me so that I was ready to drop down, but I turn'd the Child about and bade it go back again, for that was not its way home; the Child said so she would, and I went thro' into *Bartholomew Close*, and then turn'd round to another Passage that goes into *Long-lane*, so away into *Charterhouse-Yard* and out into *St. John's-street*, then crossing into *Smithfield*, went down *Chick-lane* and into *Field-lane* to *Holbourn-bridge*, when mixing with the Crowd of People usually passing there, it was not possible to have been found out; and thus I enterpriz'd my second Sally into the World.

The thoughts of this Booty put out all the thoughts of the first, and the Reflections I had made wore quickly off; Poverty, as I have said, harden'd my Heart, and my own Necessities made me regardless of any thing: The last Affair left no great Concern upon me, for as I did the poor Child no harm, I only said to my self, I had given the Parents a just Reproof for their Negligence in leaving the poor little Lamb to come home by it self, and it would teach them to take more Care of it another time.

This String of Beads was worth about Twelve or Fourteen Pounds; I suppose it might have been formerly the Mother's, for it was too big for the Child's wear, but that, perhaps, the Vanity of the Mother to have her Child look Fine at the Dancing School, had made her let the Child wear it; and no doubt the Child had a Maid sent to take care of it, but she, like a careless Jade, was taken up perhaps with some Fellow that had met her by the way, and so the poor Baby wandred till it fell into my Hands.

However, I did the Child no harm; I did not so much as fright it, for I had a great many tender Thoughts about me yet, and did nothing but what, as I may say, meer Necessity drove me to.

This is a dark passage, in which Moll frightens herself by her recognition that she has contemplated murder, however briefly. We have learned in a preceding paragraph that she interprets her compulsion to embark on a new crime as the work of 'an evil Counsellor within', and it is this 'Devil' which prompts her to identify an unaccompanied child as a potential victim. The 'Child' – a daughter of wealthy parents who send her to 'Dancing-School' – is presented as a predator sees its helpless prey: 'a pretty little Child', 'this innocent Creature'. The reader fears for the trusting little girl, as Moll gains her confidence, so that 'it prattl'd' to her as she 'took it by the Hand' and led her into a dark alley. Moll deftly removes the gold necklace which caught her eye in the first place, by pretending to re-fasten the girl's shoe (a 'Clog', probably a thick-soled outer shoe that the child wore in the muddy streets, perhaps over her dancing shoes). Although Moll is skilful enough to steal the necklace without the child's being aware of the loss, and lets the reader know about her dexterity, she now feels herself to be in danger with the stolen gold beads in her possession, and says 'the Devil put me upon killing the Child in the dark Alley, that it might not Cry'. Perhaps the child is unwittingly near to death for a moment, but Moll's 'very thought' of killing the child

ACT 2 continued

to secure her escape frightened her so that she 'was ready to drop down'. Moll is prepared to admit to a great deal of wickedness, but she wants us to know that she is not a murderess.

Moll describes her getaway, demonstrating her frequent practice of rapidly taking a circuitous route away from the scene of the crime and then mixing with a crowd, where 'it was not possible to have been found out'. There is a familiar, self-congratulatory note in the way she says '... thus I enterpriz'd my second Sally into the World'.

As usual, a passage of accusations and excuses follows the exploit. Moll makes much of having taught the child's parents a lesson – giving them 'a just Reproof for their Negligence in leaving the poor little Lamb to come home by it self'. She invents a theory that it must have been vanity that led the child's mother to give it her own – too large – necklace to wear, to 'look Fine at the Dancing-School', and imagines that a maid must have been sent to meet the little girl but that the 'careless Jade' had perhaps met 'some Fellow' on the way and neglected her duty to the 'poor Babe'. This sanctimonious interpretation of events by one who – however briefly – has contemplated murdering the child, strikes the reader as hypocritical, to say the least. Moll's final justification is that the child was unharmed and not even scared, since she was still subject to 'many tender Thoughts' (as a mother of young children, presumably), and – her usual claim at this stage of her career as a thief – was driven by 'meer Necessity'.

TEXT 3   (PP. 325–7)

Moll's successful, even triumphant career as a thief has made her prosperous. But she is unable to give up her criminal ways and the following extract marks the beginning of the inevitable decline in her fortunes:

> I was now in good Circumstances indeed, if I could have known my time for leaving off, and my Governess often said I was the richest of the Trade in *England*, and so I believe I was; for I had 700 *l.* by me in Money, besides Cloaths, Rings, some Plate, and two gold Watches, and all of them stol'n, for I had innumerable Jobbs besides these I have mention'd; O! had I even now had the Grace of Repentance, I had still leisure to have look'd back upon my Follies, and have made

some Reparation; but the satisfaction I was to make for the publick Mischiefs I
had done, was yet left behind; and I could not forbear going Abroad again, *as
I call'd it now*, any more than I could when my Extremity really drove me out for
Bread.

It was not long after the affair with the *Mercer* was made up, that I went out in an
Equipage quite different from any I had ever appear'd in before; I dress'd myself
like a Beggar Woman, in the coarsest and most despicable Rags I could get, and I
walk'd about peering, and peeping into every Door and Window I came near; and
indeed I was in such a Plight now, that I knew as ill how to behave in as ever I did
in any; I naturally abhorr'd Dirt and Rags; I had been bred up Tite and Cleanly,
and could be no other, what ever Condition I was in; so that this was the most
uneasie Disguise to me that ever I put on. I said presently to myself that this would
not do, for this was a Dress that every body was shy, and afraid of; and I thought
every body look'd at me, as if they were afraid I should come near them, lest I
should take something from them, or afraid to come near me, lest they should get
something from me: I wandered about all the Evening the first time I went out,
and made nothing of it, but came home again wet, draggl'd and tired; However I
went out again, the next Night, and then I met with a little Adventure, which had
like to have cost me dear; as I was standing near a Tavern Door, there comes a
Gentleman on Horse back, and lights at the Door, and wanting to go into the
Tavern, he calls one of the Drawers to hold his Horse; he stay'd pretty long in the
Tavern, and the Drawer heard his Master call, and thought he would be angry
with him; seeing me stand by him, he call'd to me, here Woman, *says he,* hold this
Horse a while, till I go in, if the Gentleman comes, he'll give you something; *yes
says I,* and takes the Horse and walks off with him very soberly, and carry'd him to
my Governess.

This had been a Booty to those that had understood it; but never was poor Thief
more at a loss to know what to do with any thing that was stolen; for when I came
home, my Governess was quite confounded, and what to do with the Creature, we
neither of us knew; to send him to a Stable was doing nothing, for it was certain
that publick Notice would be given in the *Gazette*, and the Horse describ'd, so that
we durst not go to fetch it again.

All the remedy we had for this unlucky Adventure was to go and set up the Horse
at an Inn, and sent a Note by a Porter to the Tavern, that the Gentleman's Horse
that was lost such a time, was left at such an Inn, and that he might be had there;
that the poor Woman that held him, having led him about the Street, not being

able to lead him back again, had left him there; we might have waited till the
owner had publish'd, and offer'd a Reward, but we did not care to venture the
receiving the Reward.

So this was a Robbery and no Robbery, for little was lost by it, and nothing was
got by it, and I was quite Sick of going out in a Beggar's dress, it did not answer at
all, and besides I thought it was Ominous and Threatning.

At the beginning of this extract, Moll draws up one of her familiar
balance sheets. The sum of her ill-gotten gains represents a considerable
amount in the context of the period – quite enough for Moll to live on
modestly but comfortably. But her success as a thief – she believes herself
to be 'the richest of the Trade in *England*' – draws her on to further
exploits in spite of the removal of her fear of poverty.

Her self-accusations about her lack of 'the Grace of Repentance',
her 'Follies' and the need for 'Reparation' may or may not be heartfelt,
but their force is in any case diminished by her more worldly regret
at the beginning of this extract that she would have been 'in good
Circumstances indeed' if she had known her 'time for leaving off'.

This passage, however, marks a shift in Moll's criminal career; there
are suggestions that she is on the downward path. She refers to her
subsequent arrest and sentence: 'the satisfaction I was to make for the
publick Mischiefs ... was yet left behind'. There are several successful as
well as unsuccessful adventures yet to come, but this incident has an air
of foreboding about it. We know that Moll employs disguises – even
during one spell dressing as a man – but there does seem to be something
'Ominous and Threatning', as she says later, about her wearing
'despicable Rags'. Moll has been bred up 'Tite and Cleanly' and it goes
against the grain for her to abandon her trim and clean appearance and
to prowl around the streets as a dirty 'Beggar Woman'. She applies herself
to acting the part, nonetheless, 'peering, and peeping into every Door and
Window', and frightening passers-by, who fear theft or contamination.
She makes a joke about this in unusually elegant terms: 'they were afraid
I should come near them, lest I should take something from them, or
afraid to come near me, lest they should get something from me'.

The loathsome disguise, which Moll somewhat perversely chooses,
has an uneasy aspect to it, echoed by the pointlessness of the theft of the
horse, which is at the centre of this episode. Moll, alert to an opportunity

as always, agrees to hold the waiting horse outside a tavern, and is bold enough to walk off with him 'very soberly'. Neither she nor her Governess has any idea what to do with the stolen animal – 'So this was a Robbery and no Robbery' – and Moll gets no reward for her daring opportunism. In fact, they have to exercise considerable ingenuity in order to dispose of the horse without being discovered.

The reference to Moll's subsequent arrest, the wearing of a distasteful disguise and the futile theft give this part of the narrative a sour note, and one which prepares the reader for the inevitability of Moll's impending downfall.

The first paragraph of this extract is notable for the euphemisms typically used by Moll in describing her life of crime. Theft is described as 'Trade'. She has 'innumerable Jobbs', or successful criminal exploits. When she goes out with the intention of finding something to steal, she describes it as 'going Abroad' – an innocent term in normal use. '... *as I call'd it now*', she says, of this euphemistic phrase, a device which she sometimes employs to indicate that she is aware of the irony of the usage. (There are further examples, for instance, on p. 328: '... and make themselves easy, *as they call it*', referring to criminals making themselves secure by murdering witnesses, and on p. 398: 'her two unfortunate Cousins, *as she call'd us*', referring to Moll's Governess's assumed relationship with Moll and Jemy.)

The style and language of the horse-stealing incident is much more temperate than in her accounts of most other exploits – there is little or nothing of the mixture of excitement and terror she displays elsewhere. We are hearing from a hardened Moll here, and one who suffers no fears, apparently, as she boldly makes off with the horse. She assesses the failure of the theft coolly, explaining the difficulties of disposing of the unwanted booty. As so often happens in *Moll Flanders*, the reader gets plenty of glimpses of everyday life. Here, the ordinary drama of the street is sketched in, with Moll as a prowling beggar embarrassing better-off passers-by. There is an easily visualised scene at the door of a typical tavern: a rider has gone inside for refreshment, leaving one of the tavern employees impatiently holding his horse, and a dirty beggar – Moll – lurks in the shadows of the night. There are shouts from inside the busy tavern, and the reader needs only to add the smell of refuse and horses in the muddy street to complete the realism created by Defoe's telling detail.

PART FIVE

BACKGROUND

DANIEL DEFOE'S LIFE

The details of Daniel Defoe's life make extraordinary reading: he was a journalist and pamphleteer, novelist and travel writer, businessman and bankrupt, political agent and spy, as well as husband and father of a family. At one point a key figure in the unification of England and Scotland (1707), he was also the author of a world best-seller in *Robinson Crusoe* (1719) and of a systematic guide to the towns and cities of Great Britain (1724–7); he found himself in the pillory for libel, was imprisoned for debt and pursued by creditors until his death as a pauper in 1731.

EARLY YEARS – DISSENTER AND BUSINESS MAN

Daniel Foe was born in 1660, the son of James Foe, a wealthy tradesman – a tallow chandler, or dealer in candles, in Cripplegate, London. The year of Daniel's birth was also the year of the Restoration of Charles II, an unwelcome event for the Foes, who were Puritans and had been supporters of Cromwell during the Commonwealth. Supporters of the established Church of England, or Anglicans, had been persecuted by the Puritans during the rule of Cromwell and now the tables were turned. The Act of Uniformity of 1662 required everyone who held public office, and every clergyman or teacher, to subscribe to the doctrine of the Church of England, of which the King was the head. This meant that all those who remained Dissenters (as Puritans and followers of other sects were called), and who attempted to practise their religion or educate their children in their own beliefs, were likely to be subject to heavy fines and imprisonment or transportation (see fuller comment on The Dissenters in Social Background, below).

Daniel Foe was very conscious of the disadvantages to which he believed he had been born: he was the son of a tradesman (about the status of whom Moll had much to say in connection with her second husband), and a Dissenter. He tried to improve his social standing by adopting (later, in 1695) the 'De' which made his name Defoe. Although he remained a Dissenter, educated in Dissenter schools when the effects of the Act of Uniformity softened, he often pretended otherwise in later life.

After the Act of Indulgence of 1672 (which gave back some freedom to Dissenters, although they were barred from public office), and his education at Dorking and the famous Newington Green Dissenters' schools, he might have become a Nonconformist minister, as those Protestant clergy who were not Anglicans came to be called. However, Defoe was always excited by the adventure of trade and by the commercial powerhouse that the City of London had become; in 1681 he entered the City as a wholesale hosier. His most recent biographer, Richard West, points out in his fascinating study, *The Life and Strange Surprising Adventures of Daniel Defoe* (1998), that the range of stockings at the time was great – from coarse wear for soldiers and agricultural workers to the finer, fashionable ladies' stockings. Defoe's visits to the home workers who knitted the stockings, and who were widely scattered in the wool regions of England, were the first of his innumerable and wide-ranging journeys in Europe and Britain; in later life, he drew upon his travels for the material for his comprehensive work, *A Tour Through the Whole Island of Great Britain* (1724–6).

Defoe was to undertake many business enterprises. He was at first successful with his hosiery business, which was a secure trade with steady supply and demand, and he married Mary Tuffley in 1684. His father-in-law, a wealthy cooper or manufacturer of barrels, encouraged him to extend his trading abroad: Defoe bought wine, spirits and tobacco, as well as textiles, from Portugal and America, for re-sale in the British Isles.

BANKRUPTCY AND PRISON

The shipping of goods was a hazardous business (as Moll discovers when her valuable tobacco cargo is damaged on its journey to Bristol) and Defoe suffered many losses, including the capture by a French privateer of a ship in which he was a major shareholder. Instead of retrenching, and relying on the steady hosiery trade, he fell ever deeper into debt as he ventured into more and more precarious enterprises in an attempt to recoup his losses. In 1692 he bought seventy civet cats, intending to follow the Dutch practice of making scent from the musk which could be obtained from their anal glands; he also invested in a diving bell enterprise, whereby a company was formed to search for sunken treasure, which was potentially plentiful, given the heavy losses of shipping of the time. But this was the year in which his creditors finally acted: his cats were seized before they could produce any musk, the diving bell company failed, and Defoe was made bankrupt for the huge sum of £17,000, and imprisoned.

Defoe suffered great remorse for his folly, in particular for its effects upon his always supportive wife, whose dowry he had squandered. He had not been involved in any actual fraud, but he believed he had behaved discreditably. An air of financial anxiety hangs over much of his fiction, not least in *Moll Flanders*, whose heroine's apprehension of impending poverty pervades the narrative. His experience of imprisonment was painful, too, although the conditions in the debtors' prisons to which he was committed at this first bankruptcy – the Fleet and the King's Bench – were not as fearful as those endured by Moll in Newgate, and by himself later.

After a settlement with his creditors, Defoe was left with a small but successful brick and tile works which he had established earlier. Trade was in his blood, it seemed, and he was unable to resist various business ventures throughout the remainder of his life: he tried horse trading and tablecloth manufacture in Scotland, for instance; tile factories at different times, and trade in timber, grain, textiles, and even oysters and anchovies, his recent biographer, Richard West, has discovered. He was never successful for long in his business ventures and his last years, in particular, were spent dodging his creditors. However, in the 1690s he had a family to support and needed more than the small income from his brick-works. At various times he secured small profitable posts, through friends, such as that of manager/trustee for private lotteries, or that of glass tax officer, collecting the duty on glasses and bottles. He profited, too, from his work as what would now be called public relations officer for William III.

JOURNALIST AND POLITICAL AGENT

But from this time onwards, much of Defoe's earnings came from his pen: he turned pamphleteer, journalist and, quite late in life, writer of the fictional narratives for which he is celebrated today. His first pamphlets were political and his daring put him in some danger. After the death of Charles II in 1685, his brother, James II, acceded to the throne; Charles had been suspected of Catholic tendencies and James was not only a Roman Catholic but very much allied to the traditional enemy, the French King. There had been much religious persecution in Britain since the reign of Henry VIII, which saw Catholics and Protestants suffering in turn, and trouble loomed again. Defoe took part as a volunteer soldier in the Rebellion of the Duke of Monmouth (illegitimate son of Charles II) against the Catholic King, which was bloodily put down after the battle of Sedgmoor in 1685. Hundreds of rebels were hunted down and hanged, but Defoe somehow escaped. Richard West suggests that because he had a horse and justification (as a trader) for being in the West Country, which was the region of the rising, he was able to avoid capture or questioning in the months after the first attempt to depose James II. The Glorious Revolution of 1688 finally saw the overthrow of the feared and disliked James. King William of Orange, who had something of a claim to the British throne since he was married to Mary, daughter of Charles II, and who feared a formal alliance against himself by the English and French, landed at Brixham in Devonshire. Defoe joined the forces of the Dutch Protestant who became William III as they marched to London; Defoe fought for him, admired him as a soldier and statesman, and was always actively loyal to him. He met the King and Queen Mary on several occasions, and some of his first pamphlets – on trade, politics and religion – were prompted and paid for by the King. Traditionally, these pamphlets and tracts, of which there were many each year, were published anonymously and it was not until Defoe published his satirical poem, *The True-Born Englishman* (1700), that his name became known to the public at large. These verses made him famous. The occasion was a reply to a particularly xenophobic attack in verse by John Tutchin (later a rival editor) upon the Dutch born William III as a foreign ruler. Defoe's spirited and entertaining response mocks the chauvinist English for their failure to recognise that they are themselves a mongrel race, a mixture of invading Romans, Saxons, Danes, Scots and Irish, Norman and so on:

From this amphibious, ill-born mob began
That vain, ill-natured thing an Englishman

he writes, light-heartedly rebuking his fellow countrymen (in the prose introduction) for being, 'particularly to strangers, the churliest people alive' (187–8).

The True-Born Englishman was a best-seller, going to forty editions in the first half of the eighteenth century, and during most of his lifetime it was the work for which he was best known, his fame as a novelist coming later.

PRISON AGAIN – AND THREE DAYS IN THE PILLORY

The publishing of another satirical pamphlet, in 1702, resulted in prison and the pillory for Defoe. His patron, King William III, who was generally for religious toleration, had died at the end of 1701, and to the country's relief his successor, Queen Anne, upheld his Protestant views and resistance to French domination, even though she was the daughter of the Roman Catholic James II. Some leading Church of England clergymen, seeing that the Catholics, who had in recent years been their main cause for concern, offered no immediate threat to the succession, turned their attention once more to the Dissenters – Protestants outside the Church of England. Defoe himself – still a stalwart Dissenter – had in a pamphlet of 1698 criticised his fellow members for their compliance with the Test Act of 1673, which, during the relaxed reign of William III, had allowed them to take up public office and to attend their own places of worship once a week, so long as they took Communion in accordance with the rites of the Church of England. It was thus perhaps Defoe's own censure of those of his fellow Dissenters who were prepared to compromise their beliefs for the sake of public advancement which led the way for the Church of England clergy's intolerance, as they took the opportunity to tighten their grasp on the official religion of the country. He retaliated against the extremists among those Anglicans who wished to see dissent suppressed with *The Shortest Way with Dissenters* (1702). This was a work of heavy irony, satirising the clergy and Tory politicians (who demanded heavy penalties against active Dissenters) by proposing that only a widespread application of the death sentence or transportation would solve the problem. He offended both leading Dissenters and powerful national figures, and this reckless attack resulted, in late December of 1702, in the issuing of a warrant for Defoe's arrest for 'high crime and misdemeanour'. Defoe went into hiding and his biographer, Richard West, quotes from the description published of the wanted man: 'He is a middle siz'd spare man, about forty years old, of a brown complexion, and dark brown-coloured hair, but wears a wig; a hooked nose, a sharp chin, grey eyes and a large mole near his mouth.' Defoe was finally apprehended in May of the following year and brought to trial on 7 July, 1703, but not before he had rashly issued more libellous material, in some cases attacking those who were likely to try him. The trial was a muddle, in which he pleaded guilty to the charge of 'seditious libel', although his purpose in *The Shortest Way* had been to protest against the Test Act and the resulting hypocrisy. It was believed by his accusers that he was one conspirator amongst many in a plot against the State, but he refused to name any real or imaginary fellow conspirators.

His sentence was severe: three days in the pillory, a fine of about £130 and he was to stay in prison for an indeterminate time. He had already spent some time in Newgate prison and was to spend longer; this was a much worse experience than he had earlier endured in the less barbaric surroundings of the debtors' prisons; nevertheless, in prison in the weeks before his public punishment, he wrote and had printed *A Hymn to the Pillory*, which was sold to the onlookers of his ordeal at three different sites in London on the last three days of July, as he stood with his head and arms protruding through the wooden structure of the pillory. The removal of the prisoner's ears was no longer a routine part of the punishment, but the ordeal of the pillory was greatly dreaded, since the spectators were at liberty to pelt the victim with stones, or with rotten fruit and vegetables, and the criminal was sometimes left near to death. But Defoe's defiant satirical poem, and his refusal to incriminate anyone else in his supposed plot, won the hearts of the London curious who stood by and they cheered him on each occasion, and even, it has been suggested, threw flowers at him.

In spite of the friendly reception he was accorded during the three days in which he stood in the pillory, the experience of dreadful prison conditions and more financial ruin left him a changed man. There is no doubt he drew upon his own incarceration in Newgate for Moll's compelling descriptions of its horrors, and the fear of the poverty thrust yet again upon himself and his growing family is frequently echoed, too, in *Moll Flanders*.

His spell in prison brought about the failure of his brick-works, which had been bringing in a steady income, and threw him even more urgently upon the earnings of his pen. His name was now known, but – marked by his trial and punishment – he withdrew into himself and henceforth led a very secretive and private life, sometimes on the run from real or fancied ill-wishers or creditors.

INNOVATIVE JOURNALISM IN HIS REVIEW

From 1704 until 1713, Defoe published his *Review* three times a week, writing most of the contents himself. Beginning as *A Weekly Review of the Affairs of France*, it went through various changes to become *A Review of the State of the British Nation* in 1707. This was essentially a trade paper, dealing with commercial interests, but Defoe recognised the importance of interesting and entertaining his readers: he introduced many features which twentieth-century editors recognise as valuable aids to maintaining their circulations. He offered his own opinions on current political affairs, thus introducing the leading article or leader – a feature of newspapers to the present day. He wrote humorous articles and light-hearted commentaries on courtship, husbands and wives and the sins of the former; he also included answers to questions purporting to be from readers, in a column first called 'The Scandalous Club' and later changed to 'Miscellanea'. The style of these sections – forerunners of today's 'agony columns' – can be recognised in *Moll Flanders*: the 'questions' offer an opportunity to discuss lewd and indecent matters in a salacious way, but the 'answers' demonstrate Defoe's own puritanical views. In his satirical articles, he used devices imitated by present-day satirists, such as revealing information whilst pretending elaborately to conceal it, as when he refers to 'a Church of England parson not above 150 miles from Exeter' (*The Review*, 26 June 1707), identifying, of course, an Exeter clergyman.

SECRET SERVICE AGENT

Defoe always led a busy life, his activities covering a wide range; at the time when he was producing *The Review* virtually single-handed, he was also travelling the country as a secret agent and political writer for government ministers. Defoe's sympathies were with the Whigs – the more progressive party, in favour of reform – but the Tories, the party of the establishment, were in power, and Defoe had been befriended by the moderate Tory, Robert Harley, Lord Oxford, who had secured his release from prison after the libel case. The loyalty which Defoe had given to William III he now gave to Harley. The Secretary of State had a Nonconformist background like that of Defoe and had entered politics as a Whig. Although he had become an Anglican and a Tory, he was not an extremist in politics or religion. Defoe found himself in sympathy with many of his aims and became invaluable as one of several of his Secret Service agents – the poet and author of *Gulliver's Travels*, Jonathan Swift, was another. The agents were required to gather intelligence in England which provided Harley with ammunition in parliament. Harley was concerned particularly with the dangers associated with the bad relationship that existed between England and Scotland – the latter always suspected of harbouring Jacobite plotters, i.e. those who wished to see a return of the Stuart Catholic succession. Harley was working for political union with Scotland, a separate state at that time. His plans came to fruition with the parliamentary Act of 1707, providing for the Union of England and Scotland – a union which survived until 1999, when Scotland voted for Devolution. Defoe played an essential part in securing this successful outcome; sent to Scotland by Harley in 1706, he worked hard to promote the union. He was not suspected of being an English government propagandist, since he was known to be out of favour with Church and Parliament, and put it about that he had fled from his enemies in England; this was true, since his creditors were pursuing him again, and he had pleaded with Lord Oxford to be sent out of England. Defoe's work in intelligence in England and Scotland continued to be valuable and well paid and on several occasions Harley rescued Defoe from prison, where he found himself more than once in 1713, as a result of debt and libellous writing. Defoe suffered a blow when his admired patron fell out of favour and was sent to the Tower in

1714, deeply compromised by Jacobite sympathies, which Defoe always claimed he knew nothing of. Harley was released after two years, for lack of evidence. Meanwhile, Queen Anne had died – a few days after dismissing Harley – and the Protestant succession was secured by the accession of the Hanoverian King George I. The failure of the oppressive Act of Schism, which would have come into force but for the timely death of Queen Anne, marked the end of the persecution of both Nonconformists and Catholics, and although they were still barred from education at Oxford or Cambridge universities until the nineteenth century, they never again had to fear death, fines or other punishment for following their religious beliefs.

NOVELIST AND TRAVELLER

However, Defoe, fiercely loyal to the Dissenters' beliefs as he was, was never trusted by them again after their misreading of his *The Shortest Way with Dissenters*. He remained an outsider, too, in other ways: the Tories knew him to be a Whig, but the Whigs, who came to power with George I and who employed him intermittently almost up until the time of his death, never completely forgave Defoe's association with the disgraced Tory Robert Harley, Lord Oxford. By other writers such as Pope, Swift and Addison he was never accepted as the 'gentleman' he claimed to be, and, in fact was subjected to ridicule by most contemporary writers. Nevertheless, he continued to write, starting a new trade journal, *Mercator* in place of *The Review,* and turning out pamphlets and tracts by the dozen. It has been estimated that he produced between five and six hundred books, pamphlets and magazines in his lifetime; he is now best known, of course for the novels which he wrote late in life: the world best-seller *Robinson Crusoe* in 1719, followed by the *Further Adventures,* and – in his sixties – *Captain Singleton,* 1720; *Moll Flanders, A Journal of the Plague Year,* and *Colonel Jack,* all in 1722; and *Roxana* and *Memoirs of a Cavalier* in 1724. He wrote other fiction, too, although always, as in *Moll Flanders,* he maintains the pretence that what he is writing is fact. But his burst of narrative fiction writing was short-lived, and he returned to what he clearly thought to be more important – fact and comment on contemporary matters. His guide book in three volumes, the *A Tour Through the Whole Island of Great Britain* (1724–6), is based mainly on his far-reaching travels – although he did not visit quite all the places he claims to have done – and presents a vivid first-hand account of life in the villages, towns and cities of England, Scotland and Wales. His last works were as varied as ever: in 1726 he wrote an exciting and accessible *General History of the Pirates*; in his entertaining *Political History of the Devil* he was perhaps the first critic to comment on the heroic stature which Milton seems to give to Satan in *Paradise Lost* (1667), as well as lamenting the Devil's power to tempt mankind – and, it seems, himself – with erotic dreams; *The Complete English Tradesman*, published in 1726, gives advice to those in business which he wrote when his own business affairs were yet again in a disastrous state. Defoe wrote, too, under the pseudonym of 'Andrew Moreton', mostly in pamphlets in which he assumed the persona of an irascible old gentleman who disapproved of much in modern life – holding perhaps many of Defoe's own opinions, but greatly exaggerated. He wrote, for instance, of the success of the scandalous in the theatre: in particular, he attacked the glamorisation of the highwayman and his lovers in Gay's *The Beggar's Opera* (first performed in 1723), conveniently forgetting that, as Defoe, he had done just the same thing in *Moll Flanders.*

LAST YEARS

Although his writing shows that he could still be light-hearted, life was very difficult for Defoe in his last years. His health as well as his financial state gave cause for concern. In 1725 he had an operation to remove the bladder stones that had troubled him for some years. This was a horrifying ordeal at a time when anaesthetics were unknown, and Defoe was fortunate to escape the infections which usually followed even successful operations. However, he never fully recovered his health and, as so often in his life, was in serious financial difficulties. Apart from the creditors who hounded him, he was distressed that, as usual, his lack of money affected his family. He had three sons and three daughters who had reached adulthood, and his youngest and favourite daughter Sophia had been promised a dowry upon marriage by her father. This was not forthcoming, and – to Defoe's distress – her marriage had to be postponed. Finally her intended husband, Henry Baker, agreed to marry her without a dowry. Some members of his grown-up family offered a little financial and legal assistance to Defoe in his difficulties, getting small thanks for their efforts. His wife, Mary, was by this time independent through a legacy and, Defoe having squandered her dowry in the early years of their marriage, seems wisely to have kept her financial affairs to herself at this stage. The persistent pursuit maintained by creditors meant that Defoe spent his last years virtually in hiding, seeing members of his family rarely and suffering from something of a persecution complex about what he saw as the bad behaviour of his younger son, Daniel. Nevertheless, he continued to write and was able to keep himself on his earnings from pamphlets: at the end of 1730, his *Effective Scheme for the Immediate Preventing of Street Robbers* was published, and he was working on *Of Royal Education* when he suffered a stroke and died on 24 April 1731. He died in hiding in humble lodgings in Rope Maker's Alley, Cripplegate, but at least one newspaper obituary referred to him as 'the famous Mr Daniel Defoe'. Real fame was to come later, however; by the end of the eighteenth century his genius as a novelist, beyond his journalistic skills, was beginning to be recognised, and his position is secure today, as a writer of prodigious versatility and as one who played a crucial part in the development of the novel.

Something of the complex historical and political background of the period is interwoven above with the account of Defoe's life. Students who wish to study this background further are recommended to read Richard West's biography of Defoe (see Part Six: Further Reading), or one of the standard histories of the time. However, since the heroine of *Moll Flanders* lives a very private life, and makes no reference to public events, the novel is perfectly accessible to readers without a detailed knowledge of seventeenth- and eighteenth-century wars, rulers and politics.

Literary background

The augustan age

The Augustan Age is the term loosely given to the literary period of the end of the seventeenth century up until towards the middle of the eighteenth century. 'Augustan' writers greatly admired the classical

Roman authors who flourished in the reign of the Emperor Augustus (27BC–AD14). Virgil, Horace and Ovid were the writers upon whom the Augustans modelled themselves, and they often identified parallels between the two ages. The great poet, Alexander Pope (1688–1744), was the most eminent literary figure together with Jonathan Swift (1667–1745), the Irish writer perhaps best known today for his satirical travel fantasies, *Gulliver's Travels* (1726). Joseph Addison (1672–1719) was an elegant essayist and editor, along with his schoolfellow and lifelong friend Sir Richard Steele (1672–1729). These traditionally educated writers of elegant prose and verse, with several others, formed a close-knit literary group known as the Kit-Cat Club, and the short-lived Scriblerus Club – founded to satirise 'all the false tastes in learning'. Defoe's patron, Robert Harley, Lord Oxford, was sometimes invited to these gatherings.

AN OUTSIDER

Daniel Defoe, of course, was never a part of this glamorous coterie of the classically educated. His education at the Dissenters' schools had been based upon the Bible rather than the Greek and Latin classics; his prose style was unpolished and direct, rather than elegant; he was a tradesman and the son of a tradesman. After he was imprisoned and pilloried he was ridiculed by his fellow authors. Swift referred to Defoe as 'the fellow who was pilloried, I have forgotten his name'; yet Swift's famous satire *A Modest Proposal* (1729), which suggested ironically that the solution to the Irish famine was to breed babies for the table, owes something to *The Shortest Way with Dissenters* and the author whose name he claims escapes him. Addison wrote a satire including Defoe's trial, where a judge suggests that he will lose his ears if he continues 'uttering such notorious falsehood'. In Pope's famous attack upon those he considered weak and mediocre, *The Dunciad* (1728), the poet includes Defoe amongst the benighted ranks of those he ridiculed as the followers of the Goddess Dulness, imagining him in the pillory: 'Earless on high stood unabashed Defoe'. Defoe's ears had remained intact, of course, but to be despised as one of the 'dull' by the great poet must have been very wounding to him.

JOURNALS

In the same way, his journalistic skills, which reached out to a popular readership, were not considered to be of the same order as those of the distinguished editors and writers of more discerning magazines. His *Review*, often produced three times a week, and written almost single-handedly by him for nearly ten years up to 1713, competed from 1709 to 1713 with *The Tatler* and *The Spectator*, which Addison and Steele wrote and edited between them. Defoe could not match the elegance of the style of these famous essayists, and generously admired their work by references in his own pages to the quality of these journals. Nevertheless, these grander journals were modelled to some extent upon *The Review*. Richard West, Defoe's most recent biographer (see Part Six: Further Reading), points out that they adopted some of Defoe's features, in particular columns like *The Review*'s 'Miscellanea', which dealt with manners and morals. As Defoe had done in his first issue, Steele tackled the evils of duelling in the first editions of *The Tatler*, and all three editors were religious men who drew attention to the social problems of the time. They were all concerned about the legal and social status of women – some of Defoe's reflections on 'the marriage market' being echoed in *Moll Flanders*. All three journals attracted a wide female readership.

Like Defoe, Addison and Steele recognised the need to entertain their readers, and did so, but with a polished style which Defoe's more practical journalistic skills could not match. Essays from *The Tatler*, in particular, still make attractive reading – the adventures of the imaginary, eccentric but kindly, elderly Tory baronet Sir Roger de Coverley being the best known today.

THE FIRST NOVELIST?

In spite of regular rumours of its death throes, the novel has become the supreme English literary form of the twentieth century, and Defoe's *The Life and Strange Surprising Adventures of Robinson Crusoe* is often given the title of the first novel, in an early form which nevertheless relates to its later maturity. Critical study of *Robinson Crusoe*, *Moll Flanders*, *Roxana* and some of his other narrative fiction has brought an understanding of his crucial influence on the development of the novel, which grew rapidly during the remainder of the eighteenth century. His pre-eminence in this respect went unremarked in his own lifetime even though *Robinson Crusoe* was immediately successful, translated and imitated, and recommended as reading for children as well as adults.

Although the word 'novel' for narrative fiction was used in the mid-seventeenth century, the term usually designated romances – often love stories involving exotic or socially elevated members of society. Aphra Behn's story about the noble African slave, Oroonoko (1688), eponymous hero of a tragedy of love and rebellion, is a good example of the romance. Defoe brought something very different to his fiction. By 1692, in his story of romantic intrigue, *Incognita*, the dramatist William Congreve (1670–1729), was making a plea for the novel to move away from dealing with the doings of the great to take for its subject 'more familiar' matters. This, of course, Defoe did. His heroes and heroines are not 'Mortals of the first Rank', as Congreve describes the traditional figures of the romance, but more humble members of society: Robinson Crusoe is a trader, like Defoe himself, Moll Flanders an unprivileged woman who has to make her own way in often harsh circumstances. These characters live in a real world, and one which Defoe brings to life with the kind of detail which, as he knew as a journalist, would offer the kind of **realism** that would make his readers believe they were enjoying 'true' stories – something which was important to Defoe, who had his doubts about the morality of fiction, or – at least – about its acceptability. Many of the episodes in *Moll Flanders*, in fact, are probably based on actual incidents, collected from various sources during the process of Defoe's journalistic life – from **rogue biographies** and early crime stories, such as those anonymous tales known as the 'Mary Carleton Narratives' of 1663–73. Defoe's readers would have been helped to believe in the 'truth' of his story about Moll Flanders, not least because she spends most of her life in a London easily recognisable to them, making her way often through identified streets, visiting inns, shops and houses which are furnished with everyday objects, and frequently listing clothes worn, as well of course as her spoils – the contents of stolen bundles, various kinds of cloth, jewels and gold watches. There are details, too, of provincial life, of different kinds of travel, from horseback to coach and six, and of how a plantation in Maryland might be established. This building up – by all these glimpses of the everyday – of Moll's world was very different from the style used before in the popular 'romances', where even place and time were not always specific and certainly the author had seen no need to furnish rooms, for instance, or to describe the details of the daily life of his characters.

The relationship between realism and the novel, as the realistic novel moved into maturity in the nineteenth century, remained crucial, and Defoe's characters, with their psychological truth to nature, have offered lessons to twentieth-century writers, too (see Part Six: Critical History).

Defoe's name, as one of the founders of the recognisable form of the novel which has become central to our literary culture, stands beside other great innovative writers of the eighteenth century. These include Henry Fielding, author of *Tom Jones* (1749), Samuel Richardson, who developed the **epistolary novel**, and Lawrence Sterne, whose wildly inventive *Tristram Shandy* (1759–67) pre-dates by a couple of hundred years amused concerns about the realistic invalidity of the novel form which he is himself employing.

SOCIAL BACKGROUND

Moll is as much a figure of the eighteenth as of the seventeenth century in which her author ostensibly sets her life. Everyday details in the novel show that Defoe was writing in 1722 about the London more or less of his time and Moll makes no mention of the dramatic public events which occurred during her supposed lifetime – the Civil War and execution of Charles I, the interregnum of the Commonwealth, and the Restoration of the monarchy. Much of the commentary of this section relates therefore rather more to the end of the seventeenth and the early eighteenth century than to the period of her life even though her narrative ends when she is almost seventy in 1683. However, social change was relatively slow at this time in history – and would certainly seem so to twentieth-century perceptions. In any case, Moll – as a woman and a criminal – was not a part of mainstream life. Her early life consisted of spells of courtship and domesticity and the housewife's life would have changed little during the time in question; equally, the characteristics of the criminal underworld of which she was a member in later life would have remained much the same.

THE CLASS STRUCTURE

In his *Tour Through the Whole Island of Great Britain,* Defoe identified seven classes in the England of his time: the great (by whom he meant the aristocracy); the rich; the 'middle sort', who lived well; tradespeople, who worked hard, and suffered no deprivation; country people, who managed to survive; the poor, who struggled; and lastly the truly wretched, who lacked the means to live, and whose fate Moll always feared.

The landed nobility formed an immensely wealthy elite whose ranks it was very difficult to penetrate; apart from huge country estates, they were beginning to build stately houses in London, and held great power in government. They spent prodigiously, emulated by those Defoe calls 'the rich', the ambition of many of whom was to enter the peerage; it was difficult to buy a route into elite society – a rich man's best chance was to offer up an heiress daughter on the marriage market. However, below the uppermost class, in what would today be called the middle class, there was opportunity for social mobility. It was probably Defoe's third group, the 'middle sort', whom Moll aspired to join and, in fact, did join by the end of the narrative. Those in this comfortable group were a step above the tradespeople, which for Defoe included what we now call the professional class. Moll's husbands came from a variety of groups: Robin, a lawyer; her second husband a merchant with ambitions to be a 'gentleman'; her brother, a plantation owner who employed others to work it, and therefore a gentleman; her highwayman husband, fallen upon hard times, but so much a gentleman that he took to highway robbery rather than demean himself by work; and her last husband, a conscientious banker. Social rank was jealously guarded amongst tradesmen and professionals, many of the latter claiming the status of gentlemen, with their wives gentlewomen. The status of gentlewoman was of course longed for by Moll from the time she made a childish mistake about the 'Gentle Woman' who mended lace, and she went along happily with the rash expense of the Oxford outing, in the guise of a member of the nobility, with her second husband.

If Moll left England after her trial a convicted felon and returned a member of the gentry, no doubt Defoe himself aspired to some such transition in status. Even without the effects on his reputation of his damaging bankruptcies, and his taking up the profession of writer, he was never accepted into middle-class society.

STATUS OF WOMEN

After the Civil War (1642–9) between Charles I and the parliamentary forces, the very constrained position of women eased a little. Women on both sides had worked at fortifications, nursed their injured and even fought. These demonstrations of their wartime capabilities, together with the developments in philosophical and political theories, led in the eighteenth century to a certain degree of independence, even though, as it was famously put: 'the husband and wife are one, and the husband is that one' (William Blackstone, jurist). A wife's property and her children belonged by law to her husband, although she was beginning to have some control about the use of her money. There is a contrast here between the way in which Moll's second husband squandered her fortune with little reference to her and how, late in her life, she seems to have control over her funds in America – making gifts to her husband. This probably reflects not only Moll's development of a strong character but also the slight easing of the restrictions on a woman's entitlement to her own money.

For most women of the period, marriage was the only career open to them, which was when they became the responsibility of their husbands. If a woman married a shopkeeper or small tradesman, or a labourer, she would probably share his work. If unwilling or unable to marry, however, there was little scope for a woman to earn her own living legitimately except by going into service. Although Moll was fortunate in her position in the family that first took her in, she had a horror of the idea of working for someone in a superior social position to herself; as well as following the traditional path of marriage on many occasions, she was prepared to follow the other traditional path of prostitution when it seemed profitable.

When she had nothing more to sell, that is, when she began to age and lose her looks, Moll took a path which would secure her survival: her thinking has been seen as an early model of that of the modern individualist. Unsupported by a society which had long since lost its feudal structure, and living in a city where without money she would starve, she turned to crime. Becoming skilled in her risky trade, she opted to continue in this wealth-producing course, as proud of her money-making as any merchant. When the opportunity arose for her to make a modest living from her needle, enabling her to give up crime, she decided very easily against this legitimate trade. The means were reprehensible, as Moll never tires of telling us, but her economic triumph in an unfriendly world makes her one of the remarkable heroines of fiction.

Entertainment

Domestic entertainment and pleasures among the 'middle sort' involved eating and music making; we learn in the early section of the narrative that Moll was a gifted singer and player, having shared the traditional musical education of the daughters of the Chichester house. Theatre-going was popular amongst all classes, except during the interregnum, when theatres were closed. As a Dissenter, Defoe disapproved of play-acting, of course, but it is perhaps surprising that Moll never mentions the theatre, although there is a possible reference to a comic dramatic character in 'Mrs. Mirth-Wit' (p. 88).

In her criminal days, Moll joins in card-playing and visits Bartholomew Fair in order to see what opportunities may arise for relieving someone of his money. The anciently established Bartholomew Fair had become notorious, not least after Ben Jonson's 1614 play of the same name had suggested that it offered opportunities for robberies and trickery of all kinds. The pleasure gardens, such as the Spring Garden in Knightsbridge, to which Moll is taken by her drunken escort, also had a raffish reputation until they were better run in the later eighteenth century.

A visit to one of the spas was undertaken not only for health reasons, but in hopes of romantic meetings. Moll would have known this when she went to Bath, not really a respectable place in Defoe's time, and she does, in fact, make the acquaintance of the wealthy man whom she eventually seduces.

TRAVEL

People travelled a surprising amount, considering how bad and dangerous the roads and sea travel were. Perhaps the reader remembers Moll most readily in her London haunts, but she travels frequently during the course of the novel. Her grandest journey is in the coach and six horses hired by her spendthrift second husband for a trip to Oxford, apparently the kind of outing that was regularly enjoyed by the aristocracy. An account exists of a two day trip to Cambridge University by the Earl of Bedford in 1689 during which he spent more than fifty pounds – enough to keep one of his upper servants for twelve years. Moll's jaunt – lasting twelve days – involved 'about 93*l.* Expence' (p. 106), demonstrating that the couple were able to ape the aristocracy at least in lavish spending.

The roads were dangerous, full of holes that overturned coaches and places which were impassable in wet weather. They were dangerous, too, because of robbers; highwaymen became a major hazard in the eighteenth century. Men like Moll's husband regularly stopped coaches and dispossessed the occupants of their valuables. They were often courteous, but any resistance was met with force. Their ascendancy was such that, in the 1720s, they had notices pinned up in the prosperous areas of London, forbidding people to travel out of London without ten guineas – to be handed over – on pain of death.

Sea travel was even more perilous. Moll's husband did not care 'to venture' Moll on a sea journey too often – a reflection of her economic value to him, of course, but also a reminder of the number of lives that were lost at sea. There were certainly pirates to be feared, but the weather was the worst enemy. Defoe's investment in a diving bell to search for sunken treasure (see Daniel Defoe's Life, above) reminds us that the coast of Britain was surrounded by sunken vessels, mostly the victims of storms.

THE DISSENTERS

Defoe was born and died a Dissenter, as has been outlined in Daniel Defoe's Life, above. The Church of England, also known as the Anglican Church, or the Established Church, had at its head the monarch. There were sizeable minorities who were not adherents of the Church of England. Roman Catholics were one group, still subject to persecution, particularly at times when plots were believed to be under way to restore a Roman Catholic monarch. The other group – Protestants – consisted of several different sects who had dispensed with bishops and felt Anglicanism was too close to Rome. These Dissenters, or Nonconformists, included – amongst others – Quakers, Baptists and the Puritan group to which Defoe's parents had belonged. Neither Dissenters nor Catholics could attend university or hold public office; the tolerance of the Established Church wavered – at some times those opposed to the Anglican orthodoxy were not allowed to practise their religion at all, at others, concessions were made. The humiliation of a token gesture of conforming during one period meant that Dissenters could take public office – a practice scorned by Defoe as 'playing Bo-peep with God Almighty' (in a pamphlet of 1698).

Generally, however, it can be seen that the Dissenters, of whom Defoe was one, were outsiders in society, particularly in the case of its higher levels. Their values included the concept of what has subsequently been called the 'Protestant work ethic'. They believed work to be an obligation imposed by heaven, and saw nothing wrong with trade and money making – in fact, they tended to believe that material success in this world was a mark of God's approval. Defoe's enthusiasm for trade exhibits this Dissenter ethic; he persisted in his many entrepreneurial undertakings, in spite of his dismal failures and descent into irrecoverable debt.

A firm Dissenter in private life, Defoe became more circumspect in exposing his beliefs as a journalist and novelist. In his *Tour*, for instance, he comments favourably on several occasions about the qualities of Dissenters, although writing as from the viewpoint of an Anglican.

In *Moll Flanders*, the only specific references to Dissenters, apart from the episode involving the 'honest Quaker' in Maryland, relate to their collecting at Meeting Houses, offering opportunities for Moll to practise her pickpocketing skills amongst the departing congregations. However, there is a sense in which Moll – like Defoe, an outsider in society – makes her way as the Dissenters did, with no support from the world at large. Although her trade is not honest – her sexual morals are loose and she is a thief – she has her own work ethic and toils away much as a tradesman might. Her reward – unjustified as it may seem – at the end of her narrative is nevertheless an economic independence which she has won by herself. Her penitence and hopes of heaven would have the approbation of the Dissenters' deity, perhaps, who awards her wealth as a sign of favour.

PART SIX

CRITICAL HISTORY & BROADER PERSPECTIVES

EARLIER RESPONSES

Defoe's literary fame in his own lifetime rested in particular on his position as the writer of the immensely popular *True-Born Englishman* and other pamphlets. He was recognised as the author of *Robinson Crusoe*, which went into many editions and translations not least because it was frequently parodied, adapted with sequels and pirated in abridged editions. His other works of fiction, including *Moll Flanders*, were not as popular as his *Tour Through the Whole Island of Great Britain* or his moral guides such as *Religious Courtship* and *The Family Instructor*.

There were no reviews of novels in the press until the *Gentleman's Magazine* was established in 1731, and in any case the fictional status of Defoe's narratives was uncertain at the time of publication, since he claimed always to be writing memoirs and true accounts of events. However, by the end of the eighteenth century the novel was recognised as a literary **genre** in its own right, and the author of *Robinson Crusoe* was accorded his place as one of the earliest masters of the developing form. Dr Samuel Johnson (1709–84) famously described *Robinson Crusoe* as one of the few narratives that he wished longer; in 1775, a critic writing about 'the Lewd Roxana' in the March edition of the *Monthly Review* referred to 'the famous De Foe' and to the versatility of his 'genius'. By 1786, the antiquarian, George Chalmers, had written a *Life* of Defoe, including a list of some hundred of his supposed works, which was included in some new editions of Defoe's writing. He described Defoe as a novelist of the first rank, and his bibliography provided the basis for gradually growing critical appraisal of the writer in the nineteenth century.

There is much about the more desperate deeds of Moll, the outsider, to appeal to the **Romantic** temperament, although her passion for gentility was not a trait likely to endear her to adherents of that movement. Charles Lamb (1775–1834), a perceptive literary critic of the time, offered sympathetic appreciation of Defoe's skill in characterisation included in a new three volume standard *Life* of the writer (1830) by Walter Wilson. More *Lives* followed in 1869 and 1894, each amplifying knowledge of the writer's life and works. *Robinson Crusoe* remained pre-eminent amongst his works of fiction, but *Moll Flanders* and *A Journal of the Plague Year* began to attract more critical attention.

RECENT CRITICISM

Modernist writers of the beginning of the twentieth century were fascinated by Defoe's presentation of Moll. In one of a series of Cambridge lectures, later published as *Aspects of the Novel*, 1927, the novelist E.M. Forster (1879–1970) draws attention to Moll's living presence:

> Moll is a character physically, with hard plump limbs that get into bed and pick pockets. She lays no stress upon her appearance, yet she moves us as having height and weight, as breathing and eating, and doing many of the things that are usually missed out (p. 80).

Forster sees *Moll Flanders* as a novel in which 'a character is everything and is given freest play … Nothing matters but the heroine; she stands in an open space like a tree …' (p. 85). We understand her thoroughly, because she shares her thoughts with us. Forster goes on to make a general point about the nature of the novel: he explains how it is that a physically and psychologically realised character such as Moll can seem very convincing to the reader, although he makes the analyst of fiction's point that we understand that she is not 'real' because we are privy to her secret thoughts and life, which is not true of our relationships with real people.

Virginia Woolf (1882–1941) was a leading **Modernist** writer who developed new forms of **realism**; she put less stress on the external life of her characters and was concerned to represent her characters through the extensive use of interior monologue. In her critical essay 'Defoe' from *The Common Reader*, 1925 and 1932, she examines the apparent anomaly represented by Defoe's moral claims for his narrative and our admiration for Moll:

> The interpretation that we put on his characters might therefore well have puzzled him. We find for ourselves meanings which he was careful to disguise even from

his own eye. Thus it comes about that we admire Moll Flanders far more than we blame her. Nor can we believe that Defoe had made up his mind as to the precise degree of her guilt, or was unaware in considering the lives of the abandoned he raised many deep questions and hinted, if he did not state, answers quite at variance with his professions of belief. (Reprinted in *Twentieth Century Interpretations of Moll Flanders* pp. 14–15 – see Part Six: Further Reading)

Virginia Woolf, who became an icon of **feminist criticism** in the latter part of the twentieth century, knew that 'advocates of women's rights' would be unlikely to claim Moll Flanders as one of their 'patron saints'. But she recognised Defoe's advanced views on women's capacities, as expressed in his pamphlet on *The Education of Women*, and says of his female characters that:

> … Defoe not only intended them to speak some very modern doctrines upon the subject, but placed them in circumstances where their particular hardships are displayed in such a way as to elicit our sympathy. Courage, said Moll Flanders, was what women needed, and the power to 'stand their ground'; and at once gave practical demonstration of the benefits that would result. (ibid, p. 15)

Virginia Woolf ends her essay with an acknowledgement of Defoe as 'the founder and master' of the novel of low life.

These influential earlier twentieth-century admirers of the work of Defoe brought the whole range of his fiction into the field of literary appraisal. There was an explosion of critical analysis of his work in the sixties, sparked by the seminal work of Ian Watt in his *Rise of the Novel*, 1957, which remains essential reading for the student of Defoe, Fielding and Richardson. In this work, Watt draws a distinction between earlier forms of fiction and what Defoe and others contributed to a defining form of what we recognise as the legitimate antecedent of the 'modern' novel. It is worth considering that a counter-view of the role of the novel in literary history has emerged recently; this suggests that all forms of narrative fiction are fundamentally one. Their shared attributes, it is claimed, and particularly their mythic qualities, are more marked than those that divide them – as, for instance, in *The True Story of the Novel*, Margaret Anne Doody, 1996.

Professor Watt, writing about Defoe's characters, recognises them as something new in fiction. He identifies them as examples of what he calls 'economic individualism'. He shows Moll Flanders, in particular, as responding to her circumstances:

> The heroine, it is true, is a criminal; but the high incidence of crime in our civilisation is itself mainly due to the wide diffusion of an individualist ideology in a society where success is not easily or equally attainable to all its members. Moll Flanders ... is a characteristic product of modern individualism in assuming that she owes it to herself to achieve the highest economic and social rewards, and in using every available method to carry out her resolve. (p. 98)

That her economic success involves her in criminal activities, in which she persists whilst claiming remorse, offers a case for reading *Moll Flanders* as a work of irony for many critics. Professor Watt warns against what he sees as this anachronistic twentieth-century view, saying that it is a mistake to attribute to Defoe the 'guilt feelings which are now fairly widely attached to economic gain as a motive; and the view that protestations of piety are suspect anyway, especially when combined with a great attention to one's own economic interest'. Defoe, he says:

> ... was not ashamed to make economic self-interest his major premise about human life; he did not think such a premise conflicted either with social or religious values; and nor did his age ... apparent ironies in *Moll Flanders* can be explained as products of an unresolved and largely unconscious conflict in Defoe's own outlook, a conflict which is typical of the late Puritan disengagement of economic matters from religious and moral sanctions. (p. 132)

For some critics, an ironic reading is also invited by the way in which Moll's feelings are always subject to her practical needs, and by the presentation of Moll's amatory exploits as awful warnings. Watt claims:

> One group of apparent ironies ... centred around the deflation of emotional considerations by practical ones; here, surely, we have the rational and sceptical instincts of Defoe unconsciously rebelling against the sentimental scenes and speeches which the genre and its readers required. Another group of possible ironies centres around the amorous adventures of the heroine; we find it difficult to believe that these were told only for purposes of moral edification. Yet the ambivalence here is typical of the secularized Puritan. John Dunton, for example, an eccentric Dissenter and an acquaintance of Defoe's, wrote a monthly paper exposing prostitution, *The Night Walker: or, Evening Rambles in Search after Lewd Women* (1696–7), in which a virtuous purpose is avowed as strongly and as

unconvincingly as it is today by sensational journalists engaged in similar appeals to public lubricity. (p. 133)

Professor Watt examines doubts sometimes expressed as to whether Defoe has, in *Moll Flanders,* produced a work that can be called a novel. These questions include, for him, consideration of (1) the episodic nature of the narrative – inherited from the **picaresque** – and its consequent lack of structure; (2) the lack of anything approaching psychological analysis or depth in the examination of the nature of Moll's relationships with the other characters; (3) the confusion of time, in which Moll's supposed distance by many years from the events which she recounts is negated by the immediacy of her story telling, leading in turn to a lack of conviction in her professions of repentance.

Watt believes that Defoe's form is a considerable advance upon the artificial narrative tricks of the picaresque, but accepts that the use of the episodic form essential to Defoe's fictional autobiography means that the narrative's 'disabilities are obvious and serious' (p. 112), although he says that Defoe was 'probably quite content to sacrifice whatever formal disabilities might ensue in exchange for the absolute authenticity which they made possible, and indeed relatively easy' (p. 112). So far as psychological analysis goes, Watt says:

> There is probably no episode in *Moll Flanders* where the motivation is unconvincing, but for somewhat damaging reasons – few of the situations confronting Defoe's heroine call for any more complex discriminations than those of Pavlov's dog: Defoe makes us admire the speed and resolution of Moll's reactions to profit or danger; and if there are no detailed psychological analyses, it is because they would be wholly superfluous. (p. 113)

Watt's final judgement on Defoe as a novelist is that:

> ... he is the master illusionist, and this almost makes him the founder of the new form. Almost, but not quite: the novel could be considered established only when realistic narrative was organized into a plot which, while retaining Defoe's lifelikeness, also had an intrinsic coherence; when the novelist's eye was focused on character and personal relationships as essential elements in the total structure, and not merely as subordinate instruments for furthering the verisimilitude of the actions described; and when all these were related to a controlling moral intention. (p. 136)

Watt's last, admiring word on *Moll Flanders*, however, is that 'what is left out is probably the price for what is so memorably and unprecedentedly put in' (p. 139).

Subsequent critical commentary has proceeded from Ian Watt's work, and battle positions have been taken up, in particular, on the question of whether or not *Moll Flanders* is a work of conscious irony. In his essay, 'Moll's Muddle', (to be found in *Twentieth Century Interpretations of Moll Flanders*) Howard L. Koonce identifies 'clear indications that an attitude other than Moll's is operating' in the narrative. He accepts that the work suffers from thematic confusion, as well as the 'delightful muddle' that represents Moll's morality. But he believes that Defoe's attitude can be separated from Moll's and that the persistence of 'this oblique point of view' means that the narrative 'cannot be called anything but a work of irony' (p. 58–9).

In the same collection of essays may be found Maximillian E. Novak's discussion of 'Conscious Irony in *Moll Flanders*'. He points to what he sees as Defoe's frequent use of irony in his pamphlets, not least, of course, in the ironic mask he employs in *The Shortest Way with Dissenters* (see Part Five: Daniel Defoe's Life). Novak is one among several critics who believe that to see *Moll Flanders* as lacking in irony is to consider Defoe himself as obtuse – a twentieth-century view, in the eyes of Professor Watt, but one which is shared by Defoe's most recent biographer, Richard West (see Part Six: Further Reading). West is not concerned with the **historicist** approach of Professor Watt and his supporters, but reads Moll's story and her final words of 'sincere penitence' as the hypocritical account of a 'brazen old scoundrel'.

Also in *Twentieth Century Interpretations* may be found analysis of the claim often made of Defoe's right to be considered the first English novelist. Generally, critics find themselves baffled by the obvious success of a narrative which nevertheless fails to meet the kind of criteria for the novel such as those put forward by Professor Watt, outlined above. Robert Alter, in an essay in the above collection, encapsulates in the title of his argument – 'A Bourgeois Picaroon' – his view that the life of Moll is far from that of the typical **picaresque** hero or heroine. He therefore dismisses the criticism that *Moll* is too close to that genre to qualify for the status of novel. The picaro, he points out, although ever on the lookout for money, is a rogue first – by nature or desire – and does not have the capitalist approach to money, saving and investment that Moll demonstrates; her attitude to wealth, even though she acquires it by illegitimate means, results in her final situation as a gentlewoman of the bourgeoisie.

If Moll is a fraud so far as her picaresque inheritance goes, she is also apparently unsatisfactory as a subject for **feminist criticism**. Since the Sixties, critical approaches have not wandered far from the matters of structure and ironic intentions illustrated above, and there has been so far no notable study of *Moll* in the light of feminist theories, although the relationship of the male author to his presentation of a woman's life is one that offers material for discussion in this area. Moll herself has a life beyond Defoe's novel, however; her name is widely known, her characteristics more often praised than condemned. In *By the Light of my Father's Smile*, by the black American writer, Alice Walker, (Women's Press, 1998), one of the female characters applauds her ability to lead so many lives and, like Virginia Woolf, praises her courage as 'the bold, the brave, the brazen' (p. 108).

One critical development has been the study of the use of Moll's displacement to the American colonies as her means of a redemption seemingly beyond her grasp in England. Luisa Conti Camaiora, in *A Reading of the American Episodes in Defoe's Moll Flanders*, Del Bianco Editore, 1985, discovers an early example of the realisation of 'the American Dream' in the upturn in the fortunes of Moll and Jemy abroad. She identifies what she sees as the formal cycle in the narrative of sin (incest in Virginia), punishment (transportation), and repentance and rehabilitation (working for colonial development). Camaiora extends this view of Moll's destiny, saying that the American episodes have 'emblematized the most salient and determinative aspects of Moll's personal life: her infant roots, her filial reunion with her mother, her incestuous marital experience with her half-brother, her maternal reawakening in the presence of her son, her final complete feminine fulfilment in her conjugal relationship with Jemy' (pp 88–9).

This account of new land and new beginnings equips the narrative with an overall form that has generally been found lacking. However, because the reader's impressions of Moll are likely to be most powerful in relation to her obsession with money and her English crimes and adventures, this moral structure does not altogether fit the reader's experience of the narrative perhaps. Dr Camaiora modifies the view of the New World as a moral foundation for Moll's cycle of sin and repentance:

> The New World is the ideal collocation for this redemptive process, but the New World is also viewed, in the novel, through a merchant's and a speculator's eye – Defoe's and Moll's – as the potential source of personal wealth and economic progress. It is not casual that the impression left by the final paragraph of the book should be one of satisfaction for a successful and prosperous life-adventure rather than of regret and compunction for a disreputable and discreditable existence. In this way America lingers on in the mind of Moll's audience as the land of fulfilled opportunities rather than as the land of repentance and regeneration. (p. 89)

It is clear that there is room for a great deal more discussion of this awkward and critically elusive work, and the reader may well feel that no critical analysis has yet satisfactorily nailed Defoe's fascinating heroine; she remains, in the words of Professor Watt, 'the Mona Lisa of the Age of the Common Man', a smile concealing the inscrutability that underlies her apparent candour.

FURTHER READING

DEFOE'S WORK

Defoe wrote several novels between the years of 1719 and 1724; of these the most highly esteemed (and available in paperback editions) are *Robinson Crusoe*, *Moll Flanders* and *A Journal of the Plague Year*. The account of Crusoe's adventures offers an interesting parallel to those of Moll. Given the differences of their gender and circumstances, the two characters have more than a little in common. As a woman, the economic opportunities open to Moll are very different from those which Defoe offers to Crusoe, but an 'economic individualism', in Ian Watt's term, is obvious in both their careers. Moll, like Crusoe, has all the instincts of a bourgeois; he succeeds in material terms through entrepreneurial trade, she through the only means she believes are open to her. Each professes frequent repentance while always keeping an eye on what Moll refers to as 'the main chance'.

Roxana, or the Fortunate Mistress (1724) is also available in more than one edition, and, like the first half of *Moll*, relates the supposed autobiography of an adulteress and courtesan, although at a grander level of society. The dread of financial ruin, of poverty, which dogged Defoe throughout most of his life, is present to an even greater degree in *Roxana* than in *Moll*. In the later narrative, Defoe has a more recognisable plot, and relationships between some of the characters are developed as Roxana's history deepens into tragedy. There is a final dark deed when Roxana is instrumental in procuring the death of her inconveniently rediscovered adult daughter. Moll may have been a careless mother, to say the least, but she is not a murderess and her story is not tragic in tone, in spite of her frequent bouts of penitence. There are some comparisons to be made between the two works but, in spite of the developments which relate *Roxana* more closely than *Moll* to the novel in its mature form, it lacks that grip on the reader which the irrepressible Moll exerts.

The sheer volume of Defoe's lifetime literary output is daunting, taking up considerable shelf space at the British Library and in well established university libraries. For the student who wishes just to sample the style of his pamphleteering, verse and general journalism, however, the Penguin Classics series offers *The True-Born Englishman and Other Writings*, eds P.N. Furbank and W.R. Owens, 1997. The title poem, which made him famous, is entertaining, as is 'A Hymn to the Pillory', where he himself of course stood three times. There is a selection of articles published as pamphlets which shows the variety of his interests; his comments headed 'Of Bankrupts' (pp. 196–207) are particularly poignant, given his own desperately entangled financial affairs.

What remains and is known of his correspondence is edited by George Harris Healey in *The Letters of Daniel Defoe*, Oxford, 1955, including his last letters when he was virtually in hiding from his debtors and apparently convinced that he was cut off from his family.

BIOGRAPHY

There have been various 'lives' of the author written over the years; the most recent collates the previous facts and is an extremely entertaining, even exciting, account of Defoe's extraordinary career. *The Life & Strange Surprising Adventures of Daniel Defoe*, by Richard West, Flamingo

(Harper Collins), 1998, takes the reader through the colourful and often dangerous adventures that made up Defoe's life in relation to the complex historical events of the period. There is a practical account of *Moll Flanders* (pp. 278–87), which makes some good points about Defoe's own knowledge of financial stringency and his specific view of poverty.

CRITICISM

Defoe: The Critical Heritage, ed. Pat Rogers, Routledge and Keegan Paul, 1972, collects useful early criticism of Defoe.

 The Rise of the Novel, Ian Watt, Chatto and Windus, 1957, Peregrine Books (paperback), 1963, is essential reading for criticism of Defoe's work, as well as that of the other major early novelists, Fielding (1707–54) and Richardson (1689–1761), and gives an excellent background to the literary history of the period which saw the development of the novel.

 Most subsequent criticism takes up points raised by Professor Watt (see Recent Criticism, above), and a useful array of relevant essays is collected in *Twentieth Century Interpretations of Moll Flanders*, ed. Robert C. Elliott, Prentice-Hall, New Jersey, 1970.

 There has been little further development (although see reference to *A Reading of the American Episodes in Defoe's Moll Flanders*, in Recent Criticism, above) in assessment of Defoe's work and of his place in the canon of English literature.

SCREEN VERSIONS

Moll Flanders, as a strong woman who makes her way against the odds, was a likely subject for end of the twentieth-century drama, and at least two dramatisations on film have been made; the most recent Hollywood feature film by Metro Goldwyn Mayer appeared in 1996, and Andrew Davies adapted the novel as a serial for Granada television, also in 1996. This was a more serious attempt to bring Defoe's Moll to the screen, rather than a contemporary popular version of her, and the meticulous detail of the settings and dress is very helpful to the viewer in establishing a rapport with the period. This version, amplified with extra material by the director, David Attwood, is available as a double video.

World events	Author's life	Literature and the arts
1603 Elizabeth I dies and is succeeded by the son of Mary Queen of Scots, James I of Great Britain, thereby uniting the crowns of England and Scotland		
1612 Last burning of heretics in England		
		1622 Birth of the French dramatist Molière (d 1673)
1625 James I dies and is succeeded by his son, Charles I		
1628 Charles dissolves the third parliament of his reign after a year of confrontations, and rapidly loses favour		**1628** Birth of the English writer and Puritan minister John Bunyan, author of *The Pilgrim's Progress,* one of the most famous religious allegories in the English language (d 1688)
		1631 Birth of the English poet, dramatist and critic, John Dryden, who was the leading literary figure of the Restoration (d 1700)
		1637 English dramatist Ben Jonson dies; French philosopher René Descartes publishes his *Discours de la Méthode* in which he 'proves' the existence of God
1642-9 Civil War breaks out in England between Charles's royalist forces (Cavaliers) and the parliamentary army (Roundheads) led by Oliver Cromwell; the king is beheaded in January 1649		
1660 Restoration of the monarchy after eleven years of political unrest; Charles II, eldest son of Charles I, becomes king	**1660** Born Daniel Foe in Cripplegate, London	
1662 Act of Uniformity passed, requiring all teachers, clergymen and civil servants to conform to the doctrines of the Church of England; those who refuse are punished		

World events	Author's life	Literature and the arts
1666 Great Fire of London		
		1667 Birth of Jonathan Swift, Anglo-Irish satirist and political pamphleteer, considered one of the greatest masters of English prose and one of the most impassioned satirists of human folly and pretension (d 1745)
1672 The Act of Indulgence passed, giving Dissenters back some of their rights		
		1674 English poet John Milton dies, whose rich, dense verse was a a powerful influence on succeeding English poets
	1681 Begins working in the City as a wholesale hosier	
	1684 Marries Mary Tuffley, daughter of a successful cooper	
1685 Charles II dies and is succeeded by his brother, James II	**1685** Fights as one of the Duke of Monmouth's rebel soldiers in the Battle of Sedgemoor and narrowly avoids being hanged along with hundreds of others in the aftermath	
1688 James II is overthrown in the Glorious Revolution and is succeeded by King William of Orange, thereafter William III		**1688** Birth of the English poet Alexander Pope (d 1744)
		1689 Birth of the English novelist Samuel Richardson, one of the so-called 'Fathers' of the modern novel along with Defoe and Fielding (d 1761)
	1692 Tries to set up a musk-producing enterprise as well as a treasure-finding enterprise, but is pursued by his creditors and made bankrupt	
	1695 Changes his name to Defoe; writes *An Essay upon Projects*	

World events	Author's life	Literature and the arts
		1697 Birth of the English painter and engraver William Hogarth, who satirised the follies of his age; his works include a portrait (represented on the cover of the Penguin edition of *Moll Flanders*) of a roguish young woman usually assumed to represent Moll (d 1764)
	1700 Writes the satirical poem *The True-Born Englishman* and for the first time becomes known to the general public	
1702 William III dies and is succeeded by Queen Anne	**1702** Writes the controversial satire *The Shortest Way with Dissenters,* and similarly libellous material	
	1703 Is arrested in May for seditious libel, brought to trial in July, sentenced to three days in the pillory and an undefined period in prison, and ordered to pay a fine of £130; writes *A Hymn to the Pillory;* is released in November	
	1704-13 Writes and publishes a tri-weekly trade paper *A Review of the Affairs of France,* changing the name after three years to *A Review of the State of the British Nation;* works as a secret agent and political writer; works covertly for the Secretary of State, Robert Harley	**c1704** Robert Harley employs the writer Jonathan Swift as a political propagandist along with Defoe
	1706 Is sent by Harley to Scotland to promote Anglo-Scottish relations	
1707 Unification of England and Scotland brought about with the help of Robert Harley who uses Defoe as political propagandist		**1707** Birth of the English novelist, playwright and barrister Henry Fielding (d 1754)
	1708 Writes *A History of the Union*	
		1709 Birth of the English writer and lexicographer Samuel Johnson (d 1784)

World events	Author's life	Literature and the arts
	1713 Is imprisoned on several occasions for debt and libel	
1714 Harley sent to the Tower for two years for his supposed Jacobite affiliations; Queen Anne dies and is succeeded by her German cousin, George I		
	1719 Writes *Captain Singleton*	
	1720 Writes *The Life and Strange Surprising Adventures of Robinson Crusoe*	
	1722 Writes *The Fortunes and Misfortunes of the Famous Moll Flanders*, *A Journal of the Plague Year* and *Colonel Jack*	
	1724 Writes *Memoirs of a Cavalier* and *Roxana*	
	1724-7 Writes *A Tour Through the Whole Island of Great Britain*	
	1724-8 Writes *A General History of the Pirates*	
	1725 Undergoes an excruciating operation to remove his bladder stones	
	1725-7 Writes *The Complete English Tradesman*	
1727 George I dies and is succeeded by his son, George II		
		1728 Publication of Pope's satirical *Dunciad* in which he attacks Defoe and others for their dullness
	1730 Publishes his *Effective Scheme for the Immediate Preventing of Street Robbers* and begins work on *Of Royal Education*	
	1731 Dies a pauper and in hiding, on 24 April, having produced between five and six hundred books, pamphlets and magazines in his lifetime	

authorial voice the voice of the author of a literary work, wherein the reader senses interpolation by the author, which is often distinct from (but necessarily present in) the voice of the narrator

balance the quality in literature of seeming rational and fair-minded; a balanced statement creates the impression of being the consequence of serious thought on the matter in question

chapbook an inexpensive, crudely printed and illustrated, unbound booklet such as those hawked by chapmen (pedlars) from the sixteenth to around the end of the eighteenth century; ballads, legends, tracts, tall stories, puzzles and other popular literary material were the typical contents, as well as abbreviated, pirated versions of best-selling novels such as *Robinson Crusoe*

closure the sense of completeness and finality achieved by the endings of some literary works, and in general found in the novel until the latter half of the twentieth century, which has seen a preference for 'open' texts, which defy closure and refuse to leave the reader comfortably satisfied. By extension, it is argued that criticism should avoid closure and refuse to offer conclusive judgements, leaving the text available to multiple interpretations

direct speech the representation in a narrative of a character's words as they are actually supposed to be spoken, not modified by being reported; this normally requires the use of inverted commas or an alternative typographical device

emblem (Gk. 'insertion') Moll herself uses the term for a symbolic picture, the meaning of which is hidden rather than obvious. Emblem-books were popular in the sixteenth and seventeenth centuries, filled with emblematic pictures and explanations of their meanings. A fish, for instance, is an emblem for Christ, a pair of scales for justice; Moll sees Newgate prison as an emblem for Hell

epistolary novel a common form for the eighteenth-century novel, occasionally revived up to the present day. The story is told entirely through letters sent by those participating in or observing the events. Samuel Richardson's *Pamela* (1740–1) and *Clarissa* (1747–8) are leading examples of the genre

feminist criticism since the late 1960s feminist theories about literature and language, and feminist interpretations of texts, have multiplied enormously. Feminist criticism is now a significant area of literary study and discussion, to the point of being a subject of study itself. A tenet of feminist thought is that male ways of perceiving and ordering are 'inscribed' into the prevailing ideology of society. This can be disclosed by studying language itself, and texts, in order to discover the characteristic assumptions which are inherent in them. In patriarchal societies language contains binary oppositions of qualities such as active/passive, adventurous/timid and reasonable/irrational, in which, it is argued, the feminine is always associated with the less 'desirable' words in the pairs listed. Women are subordinated because they are perceived through this constantly repeated framework of negative perceptions which are ingrained in language: areas of human achievement are defined in terms of male ideas and aspirations, and it is standardly presumed that advances in civilisation have always been brought about by men. Women are thus conditioned to enter society accepting their own inferiority, and even co-operating in and approving its perpetuation. Femininity is regarded as a construct of society.

One task of feminist criticism is to examine and re-evaluate literature in the light of these perceptions. However, another aspect of feminist criticism involves the study, sometimes known as 'gynocriticism', of women writers and the female imagination; this approach requires a polarisation of male and female which can be seen as a perpetuation and tacit acceptance of the masculine/feminine dichotomy described above

genre (Fr. 'type') the term for a kind or type of literature. The three major genres are poetry, drama and prose, to which the novel belongs. These may be subdivided into many other genres. In the case of the novel, it is possible to identify, for instance, the picaresque or rogue biography, the epistolary novel, the Bildungsroman (Ger. 'formation-novel', describing the protagonist's development from childhood to maturity), the sociological novel, the historical novel, the short story, the novella (a short novel, longer than a short story), science fiction, the 'thriller', or – recently – the magic realist novel, in which realistic and non-realistic or supernatural conventions are mixed together in the same narrative.

historicism see New Historicism

irony a use of language, widespread in all kinds of literature and everyday speech, which is characterised by writing or saying one thing while meaning another. Ironic statements in literature are not always easily discerned or understood; in certain cases the context of an ironic statement will make clear the actual meaning intended, but more often a writer will have to rely on the reader's shared knowledge and values. An ironic statement on its own, therefore, is liable to confuse anyone not familiar with the attitudes of the writer and/or his society;

equally, the twentieth-century reader may perceive irony where none is intended. These factors make the identification of the presence or otherwise of irony in *Moll Flanders* dependent on matters beyond the purely literary, and are the cause of considerable contention

Modernism is the label that distinguishes some characteristics of twentieth-century writing in so far as it differs from the literary conventions inherited from the nineteenth century. World War I was probably the major catalyst for the developments which took place in literature, which centred upon change and innovation. New approaches were moulded by an appreciation of the persistence of myth in all cultures, prompted by Sir James Fraser's anthropological work *The Golden Bough,* and owed much to a new understanding of human psychology, following the publication of the works of Sigmund Freud. The most typical 'modernist' feature of twentieth-century writing is its experimental quality – a quality which has persisted to the end of the century and which causes some critics to claim that we are still in the age of Modernism, although other critics suggest that the period of Modernism ended around 1940. (This literary label, incidentally, has today nothing to do with modernity, in its sense of 'contemporary'.)

Defoe's narratives, especially *Robinson Crusoe* and *Moll Flanders*, appealed to Modernist writers such as Virginia Woolf for instance (see Part Six: Critical History), not least because they recognised qualities of early psychological realism in the eighteenth-century writer's characterisation

narrative modes and **narrative viewpoint** a narrative is a story, tale, or recital of events. To create a narrative, as distinct from the flux of raw experience, is to recount a specific selection of events and establish some relationship between them. A narrative is generally composed of a mixture of different modes of writing: a novel, for instance, is likely to include dramatised incident, description, dialogue, reporting of past events, reflection by the author (and/or characters), generalised commentary and figurative writing. What brings all these diverse things together is the narrator. In understanding and commenting on a story, the reader's attention is immediately focused on the narrative viewpoint. In the case of *Moll Flanders* there is often a sense of the fusing of the viewpoint of Moll herself and that of her creator

New Historicism the work of a loose affiliation of critics who discuss literary works in terms of their historical contexts – an important way to understand the background to a novel like *Moll Flanders* and often involving minute research. This approach to literary criticism is a reaction against the anti-historical critical methodology of earlier twentieth-century approaches

picaresque (Sp. *Picaro*, 'rogue') the picaresque novel recounts the adventures of a likeable rogue. It is traditionally a comedy and usually has a simple plot, episodic in structure, consisting of a series of adventures happening to the hero, whose character changes little; its tone is likely to be amoral and satiric. Such narratives originated in sixteenth-century Spain, but picaresque elements persist in the narrative structure of novels up to the present day. The degree to which *Moll Flanders* does or does not transcend the picaresque is a matter which has exercised critics of Defoe's work

realism a loose critical term used of literature (and other art) which is concerned with depicting events in a life-like ('realistic') manner. The attempt to portray events realistically is one of the innovative traits of Defoe's fiction: *Robinson Crusoe* (1719) and *Moll Flanders*, for instance, have a specificity of time and place and are full of detail of everyday life, features then new to the narrative and upon which one of the claims for Defoe's role as the first novelist are founded. By the middle of the nineteenth century many writers saw themselves as confronting, describing and documenting new truths about people in society, and the theory of the novel in the twentieth century is still bound up with the genre's relationship to realism

reported speech or **indirect speech** conversation or dialogue which is usually reported by someone other than the original speaker. Often introduced by a phrase such as 'he said that ...', it is not marked by a typographical device such as inverted commas

rogue biography a popular genre of the seventeenth and eighteenth century, offering a heightened account of the deeds of a well known criminal, usually including an account of the last words and execution of the subject. Printed as a pamphlet or single sheet, it would be sold in the streets and sometimes posted on inn walls. Defoe, as a journalist, knew how much the public enjoyed these stories of wickedness and daring

Romanticism (Fr. romans, 'romance') the term 'Romantic' is usually best avoided, since it can be used in so many vague and different ways. On p. 89, however, it refers specifically to what is known as the Romantic period in English literary history, roughly following the French Revolution of 1789, until about 1830. Defoe worked in the earlier part of the 18th century, when elegant writers stressed the need for reason and balance in their work. Writers of the Romantic period, however, valued feeling and emotion rather than the human capacity to reason and would have warmed to Moll's struggles and to some aspects of her character

satire literature which exhibits or examines vice and folly and makes them appear ridiculous or contemptible. Satire is directed against a person or a type, and is usually morally censorious, using laughter as a means of attack rather than merely for the evocation of mirth or pleasure

stream of consciousness a common narrative technique in the modern novel: the attempt to convey all the contents of a character's mind – memory, sensory perceptions, feelings, intuitions and thoughts – in relation to the stream of experience as it passes by, often seemingly at random. This technique is linked in particular with understanding of the work of the psychoanalyst Sigmund Freud (1856–1939) and therefore cannot be appropriately related to earlier periods. Many of the complex musings of Defoe's heroine in *Moll Flanders,* however, give an indication of the kind of approach which the novelist Virginia Woolf (1882–1941) was to describe, in relation to her own innovative work, as 'an imitation of the mind's experience' some two hundred years later

stichomythia (Gk. 'lines of talk') dialogue in alternate lines, often in verse, giving a sense of rapid but controlled argument, as in this extract from a longer passage of stichomythia from Shakespeare's *Richard III*, IV.4:

KING RICHARD: Say I will love her everlastingly.
QUEEN ELIZABETH: But how long shall that title 'ever' last?
KING RICHARD: Sweetly in force until her fair life's end.
QUEEN ELIZABETH: But how long shall her sweet life last?
KING RICHARD: As long as heaven and nature lengthens it.
QUEEN ELIZABETH: As long as hell and Richard likes of it.

It is unexpected to find Moll and her intended husband engaging in such a fancy literary form

symbol a symbol may be seen as a species of metaphor in which the exact subject of the metaphor is not made explicit, and may even be mysterious. A persistent use of both conventional and private symbolism is associated with the English Romantic poets, particularly Blake and Shelley (see, e.g. Blake's 'The Sick Rose'). The Symbolist Movement, however, relates to French poets of the latter half of the nineteenth century (Baudelaire, Rimbaud, Verlaine, Mallarmé, Paul Valéry), whose influence persists into the work of twentieth-century Modernist writers, such as T.S. Eliot and James Joyce. There is little symbolism in *Moll Flanders*, and it can be argued that the use of symbolism is at odds with the kind of realism introduced by eighteenth-century novelists

syntax (Gk. 'arrangement') the arrangement of words in their appropriate forms and proper sequence in order to achieve meaning

tone the words an author chooses in a literary work may impart a sense of a particular mood or manner in which a sentence or passage should be read: angrily, imploringly, monotonously, pompously, wittily, and so on. Tone is thus a critical concept which implies that literature is like speech, requiring a speaker and a listener, tone being the attitude adopted by the speaker towards the listener, gathered and understood from the kind of syntax and vocabulary used: thus, for the full understanding of a work it is essential to recognise the tone or range of tones

viewpoint see narrative viewpoint

Author of this note

Delia Dick was one of the first Open University graduates; her postgraduate study was at the University of Warwick. She has been head of the Sixth Form at the Blue Coat School, Coventry, and is currently a lecturer at Coventry University, teaching English Literature. She is also the author of the York Notes on Jane Austen's *Mansfield Park* and *Talking Heads*.

ADVANCED LEVEL TITLES

York Notes Advanced (£3.99 each)

Margaret Atwood
Cat's Eye

Margaret Atwood
The Handmaid's Tale

Jane Austen
Mansfield Park

Jane Austen
Persuasion

Jane Austen
Pride and Prejudice

Alan Bennett
Talking Heads

William Blake
Songs of Innocence and of Experience

Charlotte Brontë
Jane Eyre

Emily Brontë
Wuthering Heights

Angela Carter
Nights at the Circus

Geoffrey Chaucer
The Franklin's Prologue and Tale

Geoffrey Chaucer
The Miller's Prologue and Tale

Geoffrey Chaucer
Prologue To the Canterbury Tales

Geoffrey Chaucer
The Wife of Bath's Prologue and Tale

Samuel Taylor Coleridge
Selected Poems

Joseph Conrad
Heart of Darkness

Daniel Defoe
Moll Flanders

Charles Dickens
Great Expectations

Charles Dickens
Hard Times

Emily Dickinson
Selected Poems

John Donne
Selected Poems

Carol Ann Duffy
Selected Poems

George Eliot
Middlemarch

George Eliot
The Mill on the Floss

T.S. Eliot
Selected Poems

F. Scott Fitzgerald
The Great Gatsby

E.M. Forster
A Passage to India

Brian Friel
Translations

Thomas Hardy
The Mayor of Casterbridge

Thomas Hardy
The Return of the Native

Thomas Hardy
Selected Poems

Thomas Hardy
Tess of the d'Urbervilles

Seamus Heaney
Selected Poems from Opened Ground

Nathaniel Hawthorne
The Scarlet Letter

Kazuo Ishiguro
The Remains of the Day

Ben Jonson
The Alchemist

James Joyce
Dubliners

John Keats
Selected Poems

Christopher Marlowe
Doctor Faustus

Arthur Miller
Death of a Salesman

John Milton
Paradise Lost Books I & II

Toni Morrison
Beloved

Sylvia Plath
Selected Poems

Alexander Pope
Rape of the Lock and other poems

William Shakespeare
Antony and Cleopatra

William Shakespeare
As You Like It

William Shakespeare
Hamlet

William Shakespeare
King Lear

William Shakespeare
Measure for Measure

William Shakespeare
The Merchant of Venice

William Shakespeare
A Midsummer Night's Dream

William Shakespeare
Much Ado About Nothing

William Shakespeare
Othello

William Shakespeare
Richard II

William Shakespeare
Romeo and Juliet

William Shakespeare
The Taming of the Shrew

William Shakespeare
The Tempest

William Shakespeare
Twelfth Night

William Shakespeare
The Winter's Tale

George Bernard Shaw
Saint Joan

Mary Shelley
Frankenstein

Jonathan Swift
Gulliver's Travels and A Modest Proposal

Alfred, Lord Tennyson
Selected Poems

Alice Walker
The Color Purple

Oscar Wilde
The Importance of Being Earnest

Tennessee Williams
A Streetcar Named Desire

John Webster
The Duchess of Malfi

Virginia Woolf
To the Lighthouse

W.B. Yeats
Selected Poems

FUTURE TITLES IN THE YORK NOTES SERIES

Jane Austen
Emma

Jane Austen
Sense and Sensibility

Samuel Beckett
Waiting for Godot and
Endgame

Louis de Bernières
Captain Corelli's Mandolin

Charlotte Brontë
Villette

Caryl Churchill
Top Girls and *Cloud Nine*

Charles Dickens
Bleak House

T.S. Eliot
The Waste Land

Thomas Hardy
Jude the Obscure

Homer
The Iliad

Homer
The Odyssey

Aldous Huxley
Brave New World

D.H. Lawrence
Selected Poems

Christopher Marlowe
Edward II

George Orwell
Nineteen Eighty-four

Jean Rhys
Wide Sargasso Sea

William Shakespeare
Henry IV Pt I

William Shakespeare
Henry IV Part II

William Shakespeare
Macbeth

William Shakespeare
Richard III

Tom Stoppard
Arcadia and *Rosencrantz and
Guildenstern are Dead*

Virgil
The Aeneid

Jeanette Winterson
*Oranges are Not the Only
Fruit*

Tennessee Williams
Cat on a Hot Tin Roof

Metaphysical Poets

OTHER TITLES

GCSE and equivalent levels (£3.50 each)

Maya Angelou
I Know Why the Caged Bird Sings

Jane Austen
Pride and Prejudice

Alan Ayckbourn
Absent Friends

Elizabeth Barrett Browning
Selected Poems

Robert Bolt
A Man for All Seasons

Harold Brighouse
Hobson's Choice

Charlotte Brontë
Jane Eyre

Emily Brontë
Wuthering Heights

Shelagh Delaney
A Taste of Honey

Charles Dickens
David Copperfield

Charles Dickens
Great Expectations

Charles Dickens
Hard Times

Charles Dickens
Oliver Twist

Roddy Doyle
Paddy Clarke Ha Ha Ha

George Eliot
Silas Marner

George Eliot
The Mill on the Floss

Anne Frank
The Diary of Anne Frank

William Golding
Lord of the Flies

Oliver Goldsmith
She Stoops To Conquer

Willis Hall
The Long and the Short and the Tall

Thomas Hardy
Far from the Madding Crowd

Thomas Hardy
The Mayor of Casterbridge

Thomas Hardy
Tess of the d'Urbervilles

Thomas Hardy
The Withered Arm and other Wessex Tales

L.P. Hartley
The Go-Between

Seamus Heaney
Selected Poems

Susan Hill
I'm the King of the Castle

Barry Hines
A Kestrel for a Knave

Louise Lawrence
Children of the Dust

Harper Lee
To Kill a Mockingbird

Laurie Lee
Cider with Rosie

Arthur Miller
The Crucible

Arthur Miller
A View from the Bridge

Robert O'Brien
Z for Zachariah

Frank O'Connor
My Oedipus Complex and Other Stories

George Orwell
Animal Farm

J.B. Priestley
An Inspector Calls

J.B. Priestley
When We Are Married

Willy Russell
Educating Rita

Willy Russell
Our Day Out

J.D. Salinger
The Catcher in the Rye

William Shakespeare
Henry IV Part 1

William Shakespeare
Henry V

William Shakespeare
Julius Caesar

William Shakespeare
Macbeth

William Shakespeare
The Merchant of Venice

William Shakespeare
A Midsummer Night's Dream

William Shakespeare
Much Ado About Nothing

William Shakespeare
Romeo and Juliet

William Shakespeare
The Tempest

William Shakespeare
Twelfth Night

George Bernard Shaw
Pygmalion

Mary Shelley
Frankenstein

R.C. Sherriff
Journey's End

Rukshana Smith
Salt on the Snow

John Steinbeck
Of Mice and Men

Robert Louis Stevenson
Dr Jekyll and Mr Hyde

Jonathan Swift
Gulliver's Travels

Robert Swindells
Daz 4 Zoe

Mildred D. Taylor
Roll of Thunder, Hear My Cry

Mark Twain
Huckleberry Finn

James Watson
Talking in Whispers

Edith Wharton
Ethan Frome

William Wordsworth
Selected Poems

A Choice of Poets

Mystery Stories of the Nineteenth Century including The Signalman

Nineteenth Century Short Stories

Poetry of the First World War

Six Women Poets

NOTES